ALMOST FERAL

GEMMA HICKEY

BREAKWATER
P.O. Box 2188, St. John's, NL, A1C 6E6
www.breakwaterbooks.com

COPYRIGHT © 2019 Gemma Hickey

ISBN 978-1-55081-777-5

A CIP catalogue record for this book is available from Library
and Archives Canada

We acknowledge the support of the Canada Council for the Arts.
We acknowledge the financial support of the Government of Canada
and the Government of Newfoundland and Labrador through the
Department of Tourism, Culture, Industry and Innovation for our
publishing activities.

PRINTED AND BOUND IN CANADA.

Breakwater Books is committed to choosing papers and materials for
our books that help to protect our environment. To this end, this book is
printed on a recycled paper and other controlled sources that are
certified by the Forest Stewardship Council®.

For Rebecca

Because all roads have led me to her

CONTENTS

PREFACE

In the late 1980s, a scandal erupted over allegations of widespread abuse of youth at Mount Cashel Orphanage in St. John's, Newfoundland. Since that time, numerous clergy and lay officials of all denominations have been charged with abuse, and religious institutions all over the world have contributed to the mismanagement and under reporting of abuse cases.

As a survivor of clergy sexual abuse, I founded a non-profit organization called The Pathways Foundation in order to provide support and services to Newfoundlanders and Labradorians who have experienced abuse within religious institutions. To raise both money and awareness for Pathways, and as part of my own physical and spiritual journey of healing, I walked across the island of Newfoundland from July 2 to August 2, 2015.

This was a journey of optimism inspired by activists like Terry Fox and Rick Hansen, but it was also inspired by Newfoundland history. In 1822, a young Mi'kmaq hunter and guide named Joseph Sylvester and the Scottish explorer William Cormack were the first people in recorded history to walk across the island. Then in the 1920s, a labour organizer named Joseph Smallwood walked about 850 kilometers of railroad track to help organize the working-class railroadmen of Newfoundland. Of course, "Joey" (as he is now either affectionately or disparagingly known) would eventually discover the power of radio and lead Newfoundland, a former independent British colony, into confederation with Canada in 1949 and become the new province's first premier. I wanted to engage with that sense of history so Newfoundlanders would be able to recognize some part of themselves and our shared past in what I was doing.

Of course, the walk was also a direct engagement with the island's physical geography and its unpredictable weather. Looking back on it now, I feel as though my step-by-step advancement along the Trans-Canada Highway that summer resembled the relentless forward progression of time and the march of history. But the emotions I experienced and the memories that surfaced as I walked felt more like Newfoundland weather—impulsive, erratic, and sometimes volatile. I had no idea just how far I would travel inward during that 908-kilometer walk. I had no idea how this journey would eventually lead to one of the biggest decisions of my life.

Memories, for a survivor, can be tricky. Sometimes they are harsh and arrive without warning. And sometimes they're like trying to untangle a knot that gets more tangled the harder you try. And I have tried to capture those associative and interwoven qualities of memory in these essays. I didn't want to write some plodding, chronological memoir. I wanted to write about myself in the way I tend to experience myself, which isn't always straight forward. I have tried to order these essays in a way that makes sense, using the narrative of my walk as an organizing principle, almost like rest stops along the way, but you could easily rearrange these essays and find all kinds of new connections and connotations and links. Reading the essays at random might even be the best way to understand what I experienced during the walk itself.

Aside from public figures who openly supported my walk and journalists who reported on the events, I have changed the names of most of the people involved in these stories or have refused to name them at all.

I have also refused to name the survivors and family members of survivors whom I met and embraced during the walk. And I have refused to recount the particular details of all the stories of abuse that I heard along the way because those are not my stories to tell. But I want those people to know that I remember your names and your stories. I carry them with me. And I won't forget.

FUEL

"You're that dyke from television!"

He was wearing a fluorescent-orange trucker's cap that sat smugly over his brown mullet. A white T-shirt covered his swollen belly that ballooned like a blister on top of his faded blue jeans, their wrinkled hems bunched over a pair of worn-out cowboy boots. I could feel the hair on the back of my neck stand at attention.

For a second there, I thought about asking him if he was confusing me with Ellen DeGeneres, but I quickly realized this was no joke.

Two hours earlier, my mother and I arrived at J.T. Cheeseman Provincial Park located approximately thirteen kilometers outside the town of Port aux Basques. We'd spent the night at the Mount Peyton Hotel in Grand Falls to break up the nine-hour drive from St. John's. And as we made our way toward Port aux Basques that morning, I hardly said a word in the truck. My throat was sore, and I wanted to save my voice for the speech I had to give the following day. I felt a cold coming on, and it worried me because of the massive challenge that lay ahead. I distracted myself by putting my seat all the way back. The sky was a deep blue, eclipsed by tiny clouds. Sometimes, I'd look out the window to my right and attempt to visualize what I was about to do. Even the *drive* to Port aux Basques felt long. No matter how hard I tried, I don't think I was able to fully comprehend what it was going to take to get back to St. John's on foot.

I had transformed my body over the previous ten months. Working closely with five trainers, I lost eighty pounds. My diet was as regimented as my exercise routine. The purpose of the walk was to raise funds and awareness for The Pathways Foundation, an organization I founded in 2013 for people, like me, who have suffered abuse at the hands of clergy. I called it Hope Walk.

Hope Walk began in Port aux Basques on July 2, 2015, and ended on August 2 at the Mount Cashel Memorial in St. John's. Mount Cashel was an orphanage for boys run by Christian Brothers. A supermarket was built where the orphanage once stood, but across the street from the parking lot, the two original gateposts of the orphanage remain. Each one branded with a solitary cross. They remind me of headstones. By ending my walk at that site, I'd be paying respects to the many boys, now men, who made a tragic journey from their homes to the orphanage.

As a seasoned activist, I frequented television, radio, and print media to raise support for the walk. I leveraged my public profile to draw attention to this cause because of how it was neglected. And I knew if I was going to expect people to go back in time and revisit one of the darkest chapters in this province's recent history, I had to be prepared to do the same in terms of my own life. But, looking back, no amount of training could prepare me for what came next.

My uncle John followed us down the Trans-Canada Highway in a white pickup truck donated by Hickman Motors, one of the best-known car dealerships in St. John's. In tow was a fifteen-foot trailer—my home on the road for the next month. My mother asked her brother to join us because he was a retired mechanic. While he and my mother set up camp, I pulled out my cellphone and ordered some food in Port aux Basques and decided to drive my mother's truck into town to pick it up. I was thrilled to finally have some time to myself. The sun was blaring like a beacon in a sea of sky. I turned my iPod to Springsteen's "Thunder Road" and pushed repeat. I rolled the window down all the way and hung my arm out. Once I hit pavement, I slammed that pedal hard, driving with one hand on the steering wheel the whole way.

As I approached the town, I saw a gazebo in the distance and headed towards it. When I got out of the truck, I noticed a small group of children playing close by. Their laughter was like music. I walked to the middle of the gazebo, and with their laughter as my soundtrack, I actually threw my arms out at my sides and started spinning around like a kid. Waltzing with myself reminded me of how, when I was little, I would twirl around in the middle of our quiet street until I felt dizzy. But when you're euphoric and spinning, everything around you is blurred and you can't see it for what it really is.

"You're that dyke from television!"

The man's voice jolted me to a halt. I steadied myself so I could get a good look at him.

"You're going straight to hell for the way you are," he added, the whiff of rum on his breath was enough to sink the scent of saltwater that hung in the air.

We all embody our pain differently, and though I could sense this man's pain through his anger, he was still twice my size. I knew I had to choose my response carefully if I was going to shut this down. I quickly scanned my surroundings to assess whether or not I was safe. How many steps to the truck? Could I clear the side of the gazebo? There was a motel nearby. I noticed some people getting out of parked cars in the lot and I knew that this one individual did not represent the good people of Port aux Basques, so I felt that if something were to happen to me, if I was in real danger, help wasn't far off.

"I've already been to hell," I responded. "And it was a priest who put me there."

Stunned, he backed up slowly then turned and hurried off. I had lost my appetite for food but was filled with a hunger of another kind. I don't know what pain he may have suffered in his life that prompted him to act aggressively towards me, but I know that his aggression and his inability to accept our differences suddenly gave me the fuel I needed. I was ready to walk across Newfoundland. I knew I would do it because, in my mind, this was just the final chapter in a story that started long ago. I jumped back in the truck and turned up the volume on the stereo just in time for Springsteen to read my mind: "I'm pulling out of here to win."

HOPE WALK:
PORT AUX BASQUES TO COAL BROOK

DAY 1

When we arrived at our campsite the day before the walk began, we were greeted by a tall man in a green uniform. His voice was as soft as the grey hair combed neatly above his brow. He adjusted his glasses before offering me his hand.

> Facebook Post: "At our lovely campsite in PAB. Greeted by the Park Manager, who said he just had to shake my hand. He presented me with a check on behalf of the staff who all contributed to a donation for Hope Walk!"

"I emailed all the other park managers and encouraged them to make a donation, too," he said. "We're rooting for you."

My uncle John set the trailer up next to the dirt access road in J.T. Cheeseman Provincial Park, across from the bathroom facilities. The trucks were parked on the opposite side to create a divide between sites. The trailer had an I-beam frame and a width of ninety-six inches. The top half of the exterior was light beige, and the bottom, a greyish-brown, swelled like a wave in the centre. Asymmetrical lines of blue and burgundy swirled around both sides of the trailer as if to mimic the wind. There was an outside patio awning and two speakers. We put whatever supplies we could in the oversized pass-through storage area below.

The trailer came fully equipped. On the inside there were gas- and smoke- and carbon-monoxide detectors, a fire extinguisher, a forced-air furnace with a thermostat, air conditioning, and even GFI electrical outlets. The walls were off white as were the mini-blinds. There was faux-wood panelling on the cupboard and fridge doors. The kitchen had a high-rise faucet and sink, an eighteen-inch oven with a three-burner cook top, and a residential microwave. The dinette set was directly across from the stove. It had brown tweed seats that could be used for storage or converted into a small bed. Justin, the Hope Walk project coordinator, slept on the jackknife couch, which was positioned against a thin wall in the common area and was also brown tweed. I slept in the main bedroom. There was no door, but I had a privacy curtain. Additional faux-wood cupboards covered the back wall and framed the double bed. I used them to store my things: eight pairs of sneakers, hoodies, rain gear, books, protein shakes, bars, and everything else I thought I might need. There was a small window in the middle of each wall on both sides of the bed. Because there was only one foot of space at the bottom of the bed (roughly two feet on each side) it was easier to roll over the bed to open the windows. The bathroom, which was the size of a small closet, was at the other end of the trailer. There was a porcelain foot-flush toilet and a small tub with a showerhead, which we hardly used because the water pressure was low. Just outside the bathroom was a small sink and medicine cabinet. The bunk beds, where my mother and uncle slept, were in the back corner next to the bathroom.

We left camp on the first day at 7:45 a.m. because I had a live interview at 8:05 with VOCM and an event to kick off my walk at 8:30.

Facebook Post: "Today is the day! I'll be speaking with Fred Hutton on VOCM momentarily."

We pulled into the parking lot of the Tim Horton's in Port aux Basques. My mother went in to get coffees while I spoke with Fred Hutton over the phone. We talked about the significance of the walk and the damage Newfoundland and Labrador has endured as a result of the clergy abuse crisis. I could hear the concern in his voice as he wished me well.

"You've got a long walk ahead of you," he said. "Good luck with it all."

When the interview ended, my team gassed up at the service station across the street before heading to the Gateway Status of Women Council for the event. The staff offered to host an event to welcome me to the town and send me off on a positive note. Krystal Cousins, outreach and communications coordinator, greeted us at the door. Krystal introduced town-council member Angela Chaulk, who brought greetings on behalf of the town, and Andrew Parsons, Member of the House of Assembly (MHA) for the district of Burgeo-La Poile, brought greetings on behalf of the district. Krystal invited Lavina Morris, executive director, to say a few words and introduce me. I gave a short speech and welcomed Reverend Kathleen Anderson, United Church minister for the town, to send me off with a blessing.

Following the speeches, refreshments and snacks were served, and I mingled with people from the town. I was also interviewed by Julienne Bay of *The Gulf News*. Forty people attended the event and another twenty waited outside in their cars. They honked as I began to walk. Andrew Parsons joined me for the first ten kilometres, and Constable Chris Stuckless of the Royal Canadian Mounted Police escorted me out of town in a cruiser. He had to put on his lights because the fog was so thick. My mother and uncle followed behind us in the trucks. The trailer remained parked at the campsite. Other people joined us in their vehicles and a small parade formed. I felt like a champion, and I was only just beginning. Julienne took my picture as I passed the sign that displayed the town's name.

I set off on the Trans-Canada Highway wearing my blue cross trainers, beige cargo shorts, a fluorescent-orange T-shirt, grey hoodie, and an army-green baseball cap. In my burnt-orange backpack I carried cleansing wipes, a protein shake and bar, two bottles of Gatorade, a small first-aid kit, an IPod, a rain jacket, a notebook, pen, and a book of poems by Al Pittman.

Andrew Parsons' assistant was waiting on the side of the road roughly two kilometers from the park entrance to pick him up. I gave Andrew a hug and thanked him for his support.

"Good luck, Gemma," he said. "Those ten kilometers we

just clocked were tough, and the fog and rain didn't help."

When Andrew left, I knew I had fallen behind because my uncle was waiting there in the truck with a fresh black baseball cap, a bright red raincoat, and a pair of black waterproof pants, and not at the projected point of pick up. I didn't want to lose time by heading back to the campsite at this point, so I took a short rest in the truck and ate the sandwich my mother made me while I waited for the call to do a live interview on CBC *Radio Noon*.

Facebook Post: "First 10k interval completed!
Second one starting soon in the rain. Thanks for
the umbrella of support. Speaking shortly with
the lovely John Gushue on CBC Radio."

John Gushue and I talked about the response I received from people in the town, the weather conditions, and how much distance I had left to travel.

"Wishing you all the very best, Gemma," he said.

Beads of rain trickled down the lone pink rose to my left; its stem unmoved by the weight of the drops. Not even the wind could disrupt its magnificent composure. I was on my own now, but the rose told me what I needed to know. Amelia Curran's "I'm Coming for You" played on my iPod. I leaned into the wind, my pace strong and steady, until I reached a river and allowed myself a few moments to rest. I took out my earphones and listened to the song of the stream.

Even further down the highway, as the fog wrapped the surrounding hills like a shawl, two white crosses stood like sentinels at the base of a pond, bowing slightly toward the road and warning me of its danger.

Later that evening, the fog lifted, and it was as if Jean Claude Roy himself painted a sun on a blue canvas of sky.

DAY 2

The Newfoundland flag stood on guard at the entrance of Little Paradise Park. It kept watch from its post. The gale may have allowed it to flex itself, but as I passed, it relaxed into a wave. Anyone familiar with the work of Newfoundland artist Christopher Pratt would be able to recognize the flag's symmetry as his signature. In kindergarten we were taught that the blue triangles were symbolic of the sea (they were also a nod to the Union Jack—the British flag); the triangles outlined in red were symbolic of our resilience as a culture and the two distinct parts of the province: the island of Newfoundland and the northern mainland of Labrador.

The white background symbolizes the snow that surrounds us during winter months, which, despite its severity, fails to bury us completely. And the gold arrow symbolizes our assurance by pointing toward what the artist called a "brighter future." When placed vertically, the gold arrow also represents a sword, revering the sacrifices of those who have served in the forces. And the red triangles and gold arrow form a spear, symbolizing our dominion over the fisheries and other natural resources. At least that's how my kindergarten teacher explained it when we were given the flag to colour.

"I'm using green instead of blue, Miss," I told her. "My Nan said we're Irish Catholics and the flag is too Protestant."

My teacher, a former nun, took it from me immediately and insisted I put the right colours in their assigned places.

In an act of protest, I coloured outside the lines and added more yellow—even back then I had a vision of how bright this province could be.

I was four years old when I first laid eyes on the flag at a Discovery Day celebration during the summer of 1980. Seeing it now made me reflect on my deep affection for the island and also the relationship between my fierce identity as a Newfoundlander and the stark realization that I'm merely a settler here. The flag only accentuates the British presence and, intentional or not, fails to recognize other populations such as the Irish and the French who settled here, not to mention Indigenous populations that were here long before John Cabot and Sir Humphrey Gilbert and every other Tom, Dick, and Harry (mostly Dick) laid claim. There's nothing culturally appropriate about settler colonialism.

I took a short rest as I came upon Little Codroy River. Pulled a bottle of Gatorade from my backpack, lifted my baseball cap, and wiped my brow with my hand and fore-arm. I knew I was still behind and nowhere near the mark originally anticipated. I had eight pairs of footwear: four pairs of hikers and four pairs of sneakers. My pre-walk training gave me the opportunity to break them in. However, though the temperature during the first two days was cool, my feet were still sweating and rubbing against my socks and sneakers, and abrasions were already forming. I would switch from the hard pavement to the softer gravel when walking in an effort to avoid shin splints, but the repetition was causing my feet to blister.

While I paused briefly to admire an old bridge along the Grand Codroy River, two women stopped to greet me.

Facebook Post: "What a province we live in! The Codroy Valley is absolutely beautiful and so are the people. Grand chat with these lovely ladies on the highway who wanted their picture taken with me. Lots of kisses and hugs and invites to Sunday dinner!"

When I was done for the day, a cloud formation took the shape of a lightning rod and flashed in front of the evening sun. While in the truck with my uncle, I revisited my steps as we headed back towards camp.

"How are you doing, Gem," my uncle asked. His tone weighed down with worry.

"Don't worry, Uncle John. I can make up the distance."

Endurance wise I was fine, I had trained for ten months, but my feet were already beginning to slow me down. I went to see my physician for a check-up a few weeks prior, and she advised me not to do the walk. She feared it would aggravate the planter fasciitis in my right foot and the Achilles tendinitis in my left. But I was determined (and stubborn).

Even during the pre-walk event at Quidi Vidi Lake, when I did three intervals of ten kilometers with members of the public to give them a snapshot of what the coming days would be like for me on the road, my feet had started to hurt. And now not only were my heels blistering, but the bottoms of my feet were too. It was affecting my pace.

When we arrived back at the campsite, my uncle had the top of a 2 x 4 wrapped in the Newfoundland Republic flag—the pink, white, and green—which, since the burgeoning of our tourism industry, has come to unofficially represent the province's cultural independence, for some people at least.

"We'll use this as our marker from here on in," he said.

The second day felt like a celebration of solitude. And though I didn't meet my projected coordinates, my last interval ended with a magnificent sunset and a choir of birds. We decided to stay at J.T. Cheeseman Park another night.

DAY 3

Justin, my project coordinator, was a calming presence on the road, even as I started falling behind. He maintained a comfortable presence, like a warm blanket, and his laughter would reverberate through the trailer and calm my worries. The minute I first met him, I knew he was perfect for this job, and he proved my instincts correct at every turn. He was looking after me now, realizing I'd fallen behind and improvising the schedule by adding a night at a midway camp, Codroy Valley RV Park. For my part, now in a game of catch-up, I had to add extra kilometers to my intervals.

I decided to rest for a few moments by a tributary. The gentle flow of the current relaxed me. I was feeling sleep deprived, and it was only the third day. It was summertime, and campsites we stayed in were booming with happy campers. Even the children were up playing until the wee hours. There was hardly any separation between sites, so uninterrupted sleep was at a premium. And closing the windows in an attempt to block out the noise was pointless because the walls of the trailer were thin.

But at that moment, this little tributary was carrying me back to my childhood. During my teenage years, on the way home from my appointments with a conversion therapist,

I'd often climb over the rail of a nearby bridge and sit on a concrete post. I would sit there and imagine I was like a river stone with the water symbolizing life passing me by. Sometimes, after heavy rain, the river gushed and I'd feel the tender caress of tiny water drops as they landed on my face. They seemed to nudge me out of myself. Bodies of water were instrumental in shaping me. I was surrounded by one having grown up on an island, but more than that—in the water I felt lighter, as if my body mass was of no consequence.

I shook myself from my brief reverie and surveyed the road ahead.

Facebook Post: "Day 3. Rocking it. First interval of 10k almost completed! A hill going downward for a change. Off I glide!"

Even though I was behind and beginning to feel more discomfort in my feet, I wanted to give the impression of positivity on social media. My posts seemed to be engaging people. I was receiving a lot of direct messages, too. I'd read them whenever I stopped for a break. They boosted my morale. The clouds kept the hot sun at bay throughout the morning and afternoon. Later that evening, the resilient sun poked its head out before turning in for the night, illuminating the landscape in different shades of every colour. An audience of lupines and purple clover cheered me on as I finished my last interval of the day and thought about home.

TAPESTRIES

The rocking chair creaks like an old mattress as my grand-mother takes her place. It's far from a throne, but on my Mom's side of the family, Nan was revered like a queen.

The needles are standing at attention on top of a mountain of wool in a woven basket next to my chair.

"Hand me dem," she orders and points.

"What are you knitting now, Nan?" I asked.

"A blanket for your cousin Colleen."

"Will it be pink?"

"It's a quilt," she replied. "It'll be as many colours as I have grandchildren. Just imagine how dull life would be if all my youngsters were the same."

"I want blue," I announced. "But what if Michael wants blue, too?"

"There are different shades of every colour," she responded. "Room for everyone."

I've been wrapping myself in her words ever since.

We are like quilts. What we know, what we learn, and what we do are woven together to make us who are. Every day we weave in and out of one another's lives through our interactions, and that becomes a part of who we are, too. None of us are the same, and indeed there is room for us all, regardless of differences. There are many colours of the same shades of human. Even if blood doesn't bind us, our humanity will. Or it should.

On the morning of April 20, 1919, my maternal grandmother was born. The bells of the Basilica of St. John the Baptist were ringing that day because it was Easter Sunday. She was the youngest of three children.

Her father, John Duffy, was born in 1888. John was an artist, and the walls, ceilings, and entrances of church buildings were his canvas. He also painted signs for local merchants and the coat of arms at the old city hall. He married Isabelle Doyle, and they lived at the top of Long's Hill in St. John's. Their children (my grandmother and her older sister) attended the Our Lady of Mercy School on Military Road, run by the Sisters of Mercy. The church owned the house my great-grandparents lived in, and in addition to the money he made for his paintings, he and his family were allowed to live there as long as he worked for the church. His daughters were also granted an education, as if they came from money, with the Sisters of Mercy.

When The Great Fire of 1892 devastated the city of St. John's, my great-grandmother had to live in a tent in Bannerman Park, along with many other people whose homes were lost in the fire. In those days, they would go down to the waterfront to see the bodies of men that died during the seal hunt to offer condolences to their families.

My great-grandmother set up a tea room for additional income, serving coffee, tea, and desserts. But when her husband died in 1931, the family had to move out of the house provided by the church. My great-grandmother quickly found an apartment on Duckworth Street, across from where The Modern Shoe Hospital is now located, and set up another tea room. She refused the dole during The Great Depression out of pride. She took in boarders, and knit blankets, sweaters, mittens, and socks. She provided hot meals for soldiers when prosperity returned to the island during the Second World War. Everyone had a job to do, peeling vegetables, cleaning, serving and so on. She eventually remarried a tailor from Stephenville.

Her daughter, my grandmother, worked at Bon Marche, a mail-order store primarily for fishermen who lived in the outport communities along the island's coast or, as Newfoundlanders say, "around the bay." She met my grandfather at a dance in Bannerman Park.

"Jim was always dressed up," she said. "He didn't want people to treat him differently if they found out he was poor."

My grandmother told me she wasn't allowed to go to the part of town where my grandfather was from.

"He had some tricks," she added. "He'd make two coats out of one by turning it inside out."

"Did he have some tricks when he courted you, Nan," I asked.

"Back then you didn't marry for love," she replied. "That comes later, if you're lucky."

They were married at the Marion Chapel, located inside the Basilica, and her cousin from Petty Harbor drove them by car to the reception. After their marriage, they lived in The Battery, the community of houses famously nestled into the steep slope of Signal Hill which overlooks St. John's harbour, and even though there were only two bedrooms, they had relatives stay with them during the winter who paid board. The additional income, on top of my grandfather's job at the bakery, helped them raise their growing family, nine children in all.

And my grandmother, with her generous and sometimes mischievous sense of humour, had a story for each child.

Paula was the cobalt baby. When I asked my grandmother what that meant, she said, "Jim came home from the hospital after having been treated with cobalt for his throat cancer, so I took pity on him and Paula was born."

Debbie was the brush baby. When I asked my grandmother what that meant, she said, "I was brushing my hair in the bed and dropped the brush in the blankets, and when I came back up again, Jim had me pregnant on Debbie."

Margie was the mission baby. When I asked my grandmother what that meant, she said, "During Lent, a missionary priest would come to church for a week and preach Christian living, so Jim went missionary on me."

Their oldest child, Elizabeth, was born in 1941 when the war was still on. She died in Montreal in 1955 after an operation to have a tumor removed from her brain. My grandmother was bedridden due to another baby, so the parish priest, who was travelling to Montreal on church business, assured my grandmother that he would visit Elizabeth. That parish priest eventually became archbishop. His name was Alphonsus Penney, who later resigned his position after a commission of inquiry, which he appointed, concluded that he was likely aware that children and young adults had been sexually abused by priests. Elizabeth's body was shipped back to St. John's by train and waked in the dining room.

– – – – –

As I walked alone along the Trans-Canada Highway, I started reflecting on my physical location against the backdrop of the culture I grew up in. It has been woven into the tapestry of my identity from three different, yet equally entwined threads: growing up in St. John's, being raised Roman Catholic, and coming out as a lesbian. When I was young, I had no exposure to people who were different. I grew up with a sense of superiority because I was raised Roman Catholic and taught that Catholics were better than Protestants. I was even told that there is a difference between "townies" (the residents of St. John's) and "baymen" (the people who live and work in the rural fishing outports all along the coast of the island). So many binaries.

My grandparents managed to see beyond the class divide that existed between them. But how often do the conflicts of our lives boil down to the oversimplified equation of "us" versus "them"? We're all different; it's true. And we should respect those differences and do what we can to recognize and address the suffering and humiliation imposed on others in the name of difference. The tapestry, that which binds us together and allows our differences, is complicated. If you're a "townie" reading this, I am one of us. But if you're a part of that larger designation, a Newfoundlander reading this, I am one of us too. If you're Canadian, I'm one of us. If you were raised in the Christian faith, I am one of us. If you're a white person who has enjoyed the benefits of white privilege and our colonial past, I am one of us. If you've suffered at the hands of bigotry, I am one of us. If you've ever felt pain, then, like you, I am one of us.

HOLY SPIRIT

"That little boy of yours is some polite," the cashier at K-Mart said to my mother. She gave me a big smile as she handed my mother her shopping bag.

"That's my *daughter*," my mother snapped as she snatched the shopping bag from her hand. But before the woman could say anything else, my mother grabbed my hand and launched us out of that store like a rocket. I managed to sneak in a tiny wave as I looked back at the woman. I felt bad for her, but most of all for my mother because she would always end up in tears. And that feeling of *bad*, when it came to my gender, followed me for most of my life.

"Why are your tears brown, Mommy," I once asked.

"Because I'm wearing make-up," she answered.

When I told her I never want to wear make-up, she cried even harder.

My mother arrested even the most confident of men with her beauty. I've no doubt they would've sworn a nineteenth-century oath to her had she lived during that time. People made way for her whenever she entered a room. Her killer smile made her the victor of many battles, including personal ones. Every Sunday during Mass, she always sang louder than everyone else, and when she'd take me to The Aquarena for a swim, she'd nonchalantly strip off all her clothes in the middle of the change room. I, on the other hand, found a corner in between two rows of lockers and would undress there so no one could see me. I envied my mother. She never felt ashamed of her body.

"Come out of the corner, Gemma," she'd say. "We're all the same here."

Little did she know. Looking back, it's clear to me now that I was embarrassed by my mother's nakedness because it revealed my own.

She would insist I wear a dress for Mass. She called the laborious process of make-up application "putting on a face." But having lived this long in a society that is still so patriarchal, I understand why a woman would feel the need to wear a mask, especially in my mother's profession, which, like most professions, was male dominated. It was her armor. Once she tried to teach me how to apply make-up for a junior-high dance.

"Poke out your lips like you're about to give someone a kiss," she'd say as she applied the blush to my cheeks.

"This doesn't feel like me, Mom," I confessed.

"You'll get used to it if you want to fit in."

From a very early age, my mother assigned herself as the guardian of my gender. She was on the defensive wherever we went because people often asked her, "Is that a boy or a girl?" I never really understood what all the fuss was about. I liked it when people weren't able to tell. I remember naming my imaginary friend Jimmy. He became my alter ego. I never wanted to go to Brownies, but I had no other choice because my mother was the Brown Owl. I didn't want to learn how to sew. I secretly wanted to be a Scout.

I even pretended to be a boy after two unfamiliar girls came across me fishing at a pond near my paternal grand-parents' cabin in Placentia Junction. When they referred to me as *he*, I just didn't bother to correct them. And there were other times, too, when I'd play house with girls from the neighbourhood. There was Tonya and Megan and Lana and Karen. Each one of them made me *the daddy*, and so as I often overheard my uncle say with a sigh after his wife would call out to him, "A happy wife is a happy life," I did what I was told, and we all lived very happily for some time after. But in separate imaginary houses: Tonya and I lived in the neighbourhood; Megan and I lived down by the lake; Lana and I lived in Florida, where there was no fog; and Karen and I lived in Mount Pearl of all places.

One time, Tonya and I were playing house in my maternal grandmother's porch, and she caught us kissing. At first I thought I was in trouble, but instead she gave us both a slice of fresh homemade bread with butter and molasses. If I knew the term *wingman* back then, I'd have thanked my grandmother for the assist. Tonya came by every day after that and told me she'd give me a kiss for a slice of bread. My grandmother's bread was that good, and it was baked fresh regularly.

– – – – –

"Do you think Jesus has a pee pee under there," Terri whispered.

A life-size, pale-skinned Jesus hung on a large wooden crucifix positioned at the center of the back wall in the corridor of my primary school. The building itself was laid out in the shape of a cross. The nun told us that no matter where we walked in the building, Jesus was watching.

"How can he see us if his eyes are closed, Sister," I asked.

"God sees everything, my child," she answered.

The nun went on to say that Jesus was there to remind us of how sorry we are. When I asked her what we were supposed to be sorry for, she threatened me with the omnipresent strap. The strap was used to scare the living crap out of us. It was brown and made of leather. Sometimes the teacher would carry it in her hand. Rumor had it that if you plucked out one of your hair follicles and placed it on your hand as you were being strapped it would cause you to bleed and hopefully make a case for your parents to sue. But I didn't want to get strapped, so from that moment on I pretended to be very sorry. Every time I passed him I'd say, "Sorry, Jesus!"

When Terri asked me about Jesus's pee pee in that moment, I didn't know how to respond to her, let alone to Jesus. I never thought about Jesus as having a pee pee before. I was told he was the Son of God, but there was only a white cloth covering the area where his pee pee would normally be, and there was no bump. Could he still be God's son if he didn't have a pee pee? All of a sudden, I did feel very sorry. But instead of being sorry to Jesus, I started to feel sorry *for* him.

– – – – –

We had just come from Mass. Terri was behind me in line as we marched in single file like little soldiers in our matching uniforms back to our classroom. But before I could respond to Terri, our teacher separated us. "Leave room for the Holy Spirit," she said.

All of a sudden, my mind started to tumble down another slippery slope. When we got back to the classroom, I put up my hand and asked, "Miss, is the Holy Spirit a boy or a girl?" This seemed like a pretty normal question to me, since strangers always seemed to wonder and ask if I was a boy or a girl, but without any warning, my teacher yanked me out of my desk and dragged me to the front of the room facing the class.

"Stop standing with your legs so far apart," she said. "It's not lady-like."

"Sorry, Miss," I offered in a squeamish voice.

"Don't apologize to me," she scolded. "Apologize to the class."

"Sorry, class," I repeated.

But my apology wasn't enough. She dragged me to the corner of the room by my earlobe. I had to stay there until lunch with my back to the class. I could feel everyone's eyes on me as the humiliation of it all welled up inside. I held back my tears and didn't give my teacher the satisfaction.

After school, I went back home and watched the soap opera *Another World* with my grandmother. That was our ritual during the weekdays—*Another World* and then *General Hospital* whenever I went to her house. During a commercial break, I told her what happened at school. She told me when people react that way there is usually a reason behind it and most likely it has nothing to do with us.

"The half of it will never be told," she said.

My grandmother's words made me think about my teacher differently. I may have been mad at first, but I decided to change my response in an attempt to see if it would change hers, and you know what? It did.

Later that evening, I looked up my teacher's number in the phone book and called her at home.

"Hi, Miss," I said. "This is Gemma, and I'm just calling to say sorry."

"Hello, Gemma," she answered. "Thanks for calling, but you don't have to be sorry."

"Thanks, Miss. Are you okay?"

"I'm fine, Gemma," she assured me. "Don't worry."

"Okay, Miss," I said. "See you tomorrow."

Whenever I had a dentist or doctor appointment, I called her at home the day before to let her know. And when I had to stay home from school because I was sick, I'd call her at the end of the day to tell her about it. Secretly, I was checking in on her to see if she was doing okay. I found out years later, from another teacher, that she looked forward to my calls.

– – – – –

My pace on the gravel shoulder of the highway was steady, but even though I was travelling in one direction, my mind was spinning. As I walked, I felt flooded with memories, and I couldn't help but think about gender as a performance. And just like characters on a soap opera, we're programmed to play specific roles. My mother's femininity seemed effortless because of how naturally she fit into her role, but it was challenging for me to act in the same way. Yet, I played the role of the dad while playing house. And I played the role of good little girl so as to have a positive impact on my relationship with my teacher. And the reason I couldn't entirely decipher Jesus or the Holy Spirit was because they lacked an overt gender performance.

We all perform and are taught to perform our gender. And when those strict binary constructs are challenged, people get defensive because it's as if their identity is being questioned (and in a secular world where human life seems insignificant within the scope of a giant universe, that sense of a core identity or our individual "spirit" is probably the last thing we have to believe in, so questions of identity shake our very last article of faith), even when that challenge is coming from the innocent perspective of a child who has done nothing wrong other than see or feel the constructed "nature" of the way we act it out. Whatever direction the gender we were assigned nudges us in, we still have to figure out what may or may not come naturally to us.

BOYS LIKE HER

"It'll only hurt for a second," he whispered. His dark eyes were as persuasive as his hands.

It didn't hurt at all.

I'd watch him from the side window on the second floor of my house as he worked in the empty lot below. His sweat made his tanned skin sheen. Whenever he stood up, he'd comb his thick dark hair with his right hand and wipe his brow with his left, using the white T-shirt that hung from the waist of his faded blue Levis. I thought those were the only items of clothing he owned.

He'd smirk whenever he'd catch me staring. The classic teenage ritual. He was a couple of years older than me. Never said much. His confidence told me everything I needed to know. He wasn't like the other boys on the street, and I wasn't like any other girl he knew. There was tenderness in his voice, even though his manner wasn't polished. When he tapped on the basement window while I was in the rec room watching television, head cocked to the left gesturing me towards the back door, I couldn't resist. I snuck outside to meet him. He took my hand and led me to the back of his father's van. He turned on the radio after he looked through the cassette tapes on the dash. He offered me a sip from the bottle of Blue Star he found in the mini-fridge. After he chugged the rest, he laid the bottle on the faux-wood table next to the makeshift bed where I was sitting. He took off his shirt and placed my hands on his upper body. The muscles in his chest flexed as I traced my fingers over his chiselled frame. I watched as the front of his jeans swelled. I undid his button and pulled down the zipper. Put my hand inside his underwear to draw him out until he took to one knee and pressed his lips hard against mine. His hot mouth resuscitated me. I felt alive.

The net of his gaze caught me off guard. I never liked my breasts, but the way he looked at them brought me back to my body. He took hold of them after he removed my sweater. His hands were like sandpaper. My body softened as they chafed my nipples. I wanted to give myself over to him. He slid off my loafers, one at a time, and removed my jeans and underwear. Before he pulled his down all the way, he took a condom out of his right pocket and told me how to put it on him.

He filled me slowly at first and moved with certainty once I relaxed into him. The beat of his body repeated like a wave. I felt him rush inside me, swept up in an adolescent tide. My feet locked in the air like a sail in the wind as my hands gripped the small of his back.

He was good with his hands and knew how to fix things. He mended parts of me I thought were broken. We met like that for two years. I studied him closely, intent on learning whatever I could. I knew I wanted to be him.

– – – – –

"Hold her arms," the older boy ordered.

"Even Medusa is prettier than her," the younger one snickered.

There was a boy on each side of me. The older one was in the middle. He unzipped my snowsuit, pulled down my jogging pants and underwear. I screamed my seven-year-old lungs out while my lower body flailed like a fish out of water. And I was caught. We were all just kids, but he was a bit older and stronger, and no one could hear me because of the noise.

The rumbling of an approaching snowplough was drowning out our voices as it thrust snow, layer on top of layer, into a bank along the street. And I was dumbfounded at how snowflakes could still fall peacefully while the snow beneath my fresh skin burned and reminded me that I was trapped in a snowdrift surrounded by boys.

That wasn't the only time it happened.

"Take down your pants," the older boy ordered. "I won't be your friend if you don't."

I was five when it started. He was the leader. All of the boys did whatever he said. I wanted to be one of them, so I did what he said, too.

Another time, he shoved his index and middle fingers inside me, and it felt like I was being stabbed repeatedly with a steak knife. Before he sent me home, he told me not to tell anyone about what happened, especially my parents, because they would disown me.

That night, I found it hard to sit still at the dinner table because of the burning sensation between my legs. I refused to eat my vegetables, hoping my mother would send me to bed without a bath, but when she took me by the hand and dragged me upstairs, I realized that my plan backfired because she ran the water right away.

The water sounded like a machine gun shooting out of the tap. When she finally got me into the tub and I snubbed the facecloth, she took matters into her own hands and began to bathe me. I jerked as soon as the cloth brushed against my inner thighs. I could tell she was losing her patience. Would she really disown me if she found out what happened? She was already getting mad at me for not wanting to take a bath. I decided to stay still and let her bathe me. When I started to cry, I told her shampoo got in my eyes and they were stinging. She filled the pot with warm water from the tap. As she rinsed my hair, the tears washed away. It was if they were never there. I think that was the first time I left my body.

When I was fifteen, my mother got a very bad cold. She was sick in bed for days. She asked me to draw her a bath and bathe her—I refused. She was so upset with me. I had to call her sister. I didn't know what the word *trigger* meant back then, but I knew there were things that would bring back memories I wasn't prepared for.

At camp one night during the cross-island walk, my uncle John filled the tiny bathtub in the trailer with ice and cold water to soothe the burns caused by the constant movement and chafing of my thighs. I sat in the tub in the fetal position because I couldn't stretch out. I was shaking. My body felt like a frozen carcass. The ice cubes plucked my skin like a flock of gulls and I started to cry. I looked down at my body. It was as though I saw it again for the first time. I forgot I was a survivor of sexual abuse and remembered how I was hurt. Not from my immediate wounds—they were only skin-deep—but from the wounds of the past. Those wounds were much deeper. You see, I've been surviving on the narrative that in spite of the sexual abuse I suffered, I'm doing fine, but at that moment it was as if my body held memory. And I remembered the little child, still hurting. I had to come out to myself.

Growing up on a street full of boys, being the only girl meant I got picked on a lot, so much so that every day was a fight. Until something switched over in my brain and I decided to dress like they did. I threw on my favourite baseball cap and a pair of baggy jeans that were worn out at the knees, took off my shirt, and paraded around the neighbourhood bare chested. And from that moment on, they left me alone. By becoming like them, I was treated as an equal because I blended in. But of course, blending in with the boys meant I would stand out in other contexts.

HOPE WALK:
STEPHENVILLE TO CORNER BROOK

DAY 6

It was almost 9 a.m. Sunlight stretched through the bedroom blinds like tiny fingers. I could hear Justin tapping rapidly on his laptop keyboard in the next room, but there was no sign or sound of my mother or uncle. I leapt out of bed feeling well rested and ready to take on the day. Once I was dressed, I made my way to the kitchen. Justin was seated at the dinette. When I looked out the window above the table Justin was working on, I could see my mother and uncle on the other side of the campground strolling about.

My mother took three weeks off work to join me on the road. When she told me, I knew there was no point in trying to convince her otherwise. Don't get me wrong, I love my mother dearly, but we hadn't lived together, in such close quarters, for two decades or more.

I took very little clothing when I packed for the walk. At the end of each day, my clothes were covered in dust or, depending on the weather, drenched in sweat or rainwater. They needed to be washed frequently. Every morning, my mother would remind me to put my dirty clothes in the laundry bag. She also felt the need to wake me even though I had set my alarm the night before.

"Time to rise and shine," she'd say. "You've got another big day ahead of you."

"Mom, my alarm is set to go off in twenty minutes," I'd grumpily reply.

At thirty-eight years old, I have to admit, I was somewhat exasperated by my mom's attempts to parent me while we were on the road. This was *my* project. I invested a lot of time in proposal writing, meetings, and training, not to mention blood, sweat, and tears since the walk began. If I needed an extra twenty minutes of sleep in order to walk long stretches of highway each day, I felt entitled to it. But whenever I'd try to doze off, she and my uncle, who also rose at the crack of dawn, would start talking back and forth.

"Good morning, Sister!"

"Good morning, Brother!"

"How do you wake up every morning looking so beautiful, Sister?"

"It's because I'm related to you, Brother!"

I felt like I was trapped inside an episode of *The Waltons*. At one point I even thought about asking my uncle for a loan of his prayer beads in a desperate attempt to summon the divine. But it never came to that. I used the highway as my escape.

When my mother and uncle returned from their stroll, we all piled into the truck and headed to Stephenville. The Bay St. George Status of Women Council was holding an event for me at 10 a.m. at the Lion's Club.

The main room at the Lion's Club was filled with people from town, including Tony Cornect, MHA for the district of Port aux Port, who brought greetings on behalf of the provincial government, and Scott Reid, MHA for the district of St. George's-Stephenville East. Bernice Hancock brought greetings on behalf of the Women's Centre and invited me to say a few words. I reflected on walking through Indigenous lands and remarked on the number of clergy abuse survivors I encountered on the highway who were from the Bay St. George area. While food and refreshments were being served, I chatted with various people. When the event ended, I went into the next room to do an in-depth interview with CBC Radio.

> Facebook Post: "Day 6 began with the lovely people of Stephenville at an event hosted by the wonderful staff of the Women's Centre, followed by a CBC interview with Felicia Latour. Good morning to me!"

Felicia and I spoke about a number of things, but mainly how being abused by a priest impacted my life and marriage to the point that it ended in divorce. When we finished at the Lion's Club, she put a microphone on me and followed us back to the campsite in her car. She recorded parts of the conversation while we were driving, my mother and I rummaging around in the trailer, me changing my bandages, which at that point took a while, given the state of my feet.

Because it was a radio interview, those sounds replaced visuals and were just as informative as the dialogue component.

Sleeping in that morning felt good, but come early evening, after walking two intervals consecutively with no breaks, my feet were throbbing. I was exhausted. The late start wasn't worth it anymore. I asked my mother to join me for the last leg of the day. At that point, my feet had swollen to the size of softballs. I lost traction in my hikers because I had to remove the laces to make more room. I used my mother's shoulder as a crutch in order to clock another ten kilometers.

The air was static. Soon an army of bloodthirsty mosquitoes would launch an attack. My fly suit was back in the trailer. I didn't take it with me because I wasn't expecting to be out so late. I wore the fly suit on long stretches as I passed through marshlands in a dead heat, but the green net that covered the front part of my face compromised my vision, and that's risky on the highway shoulder when there's nothing separating you from the vehicles clocking exceptionally high speeds. Even though the majority of my clothing was fluorescent, it was safer for me to face the oncoming traffic when the RCMP escort wasn't following behind me.

In the distance, the sun seemed to impale itself on the prongs of spruce trees. Rich hues of red and pink clouds lined the sky like the vapor trails of a jet. The day was coming to a close, but I was nowhere near finished, and there was no reprieve from transport trucks rushing by or the whip of air that followed like a splash of cold water on my face. I'd confront those eighteen-wheelers head on even though one almost took me out when I was nineteen. That day, a trucker turned into a parking lot and failed to notice that my tiny car in the next lane was getting squashed like a bug underneath him. I turned off the engine and put my hand on the horn. The firefighters had to use the Jaws of Life to remove me from the vehicle. But I survived without a scratch. Perhaps escaping death yet again gave me a sense of invincibility. On the walk, I removed my baseball cap whenever I saw a transport truck coming, and the drivers always honked as they passed me by. It reminded me of the locomotive conductors blowing their horns for me when I was little.

My mother hosed me down with insect repellent immediately after she doused herself. She popped the collar of her pale-pink polo shirt and pulled the white visor tennis hat down over her eyebrows. She removed the pink windbreaker tied around her waist and threw it over my head in the hope it would keep the flies away. But when I spotted an oncoming truck, I tried to remove the jacket hastily. Somehow I managed to tangle myself in it and it looked as though my body was engulfed in flames. The jacket eventually ended up on the ground. I felt too self-conscious about sporting the colour pink. Not only was it incorporated into every item of clothing my mother made me wear when I was little, but it was also associated with a femininity I wanted to stomp out of myself completely.

When I realized how ridiculous I was being, I retrieved the jacket from the ground. I wiped off the dust and put it back around my head. The truck passed by, and my mother and I laughed so hard our bellies started to ache. I may not have covered as much distance that particular day, but she and I sure had come a long way.

By the time we finished, it was nightfall. I was scratching profusely as I had more fly bites than usual. Uncle John was waiting at the designated pick-up spot. And as we drove back to the campsite, I thought back on my mother's gesture of wrapping me in her jacket and my knee-jerk reaction. *Why are certain colours assigned to gender,* I wondered? But the even bigger question that weighed on me was why are certain roles assigned to gender? Maybe we should be rejecting those instead.

Even though my mom and I had shared a laugh on the walk, I still felt deflated. But I took note when I saw the bright orange moon above Barachois Pond Provincial Park. Even though the moon was half-full, it still found a way to shine.

DAY 7

Before starting out for another long day on the road, Uncle John sauntered outside the truck while I sat in the passenger's seat responding to questions during a live interview on VOCM's *Open Line*. I received numerous media requests while on the walk, and internet service at the camps varied. There was no telling where or when I'd do an interview. And it was paramount that I respond to as many media requests as possible. The whole point of walking across the island was to raise public awareness, and I knew I needed the media's help to accomplish my goal.

Open Line is Newfoundland's most popular call-in radio show. In 1989, an investigation into abuse at Mount Cashel was prompted when a woman called the broadcast and claimed that police and government officials covered up allegations from the 1970s. So that interview felt important to me.

> *Facebook Post: "Day 7 began with an interview on VOCM's Open Line. Grand chat Paddy Daly! Back at it!"*

It was cloudy, but the heat weighed me down it was so heavy. Everything about the sky shouted rain. It held off during the morning and for most of the afternoon. There weren't many hills on this particular section of highway and one long one going downward—a welcomed relief.

> *Facebook Post: "Soaring happily down this hill! Meeting with NTV's Don Bradshaw on the side of the TCH shortly. Interview airing tonight!"*

Later that day, the wind hurled at me from all directions in the rain's shadow. The water on my face felt like tiny darts. The gusts were so forceful I had to dig my feet into the gravel to steady myself while walking. The inside of my hikers may as well have been filled with shards of glass. That's how painful it was to walk.

I managed to finish my three intervals, but when I got back to the campsite I limped to the trailer. I took my mother's hand when she opened the door. There was a step, so I took my time and climbed it carefully, but on my way in, I hit my left foot off the dinette seat and wailed in agony.

"Jesus Christ!" I cried out.

"Gem, if you're going to take the Lord's name in vain, please let me know so I can leave the trailer," said my uncle.

"It's not something I can foresee, Uncle John, because

of how it comes over me. It's as if the Holy Spirit fills me up to the point that I need to utter Jesus's name like in a prayer," I responded.

He didn't buy it.

"I'm just worried about your soul, Gem."

"But, don't you think God will give me a pass for doing this walk?"

"Maybe for today, Gem."

He went to his bunk in the corner of the trailer and prayed a rosary.

It took some practice, but after saying, "Cheese is diced," about forty times, I was converted.

Uncle John is a devout Catholic. There have been times when I'd be marching with a group of people who were Pro-Choice at the very same time he was protesting with a group of people who were Pro-Life. My cousin told me that before they left the house to attend my wedding to my ex-wife, my uncle put his jacket on and then took it off at least five times before deciding to leave the house. But I understood that. As a queer person living in a heteronormative world, it's difficult to push beyond yourself and go to spaces where you're uncomfortable. He was experiencing a similar discomfort, and he did that out of love for me. And if he had any reservations about spending three weeks in close quarters with Justin, a gay man, I certainly couldn't tell. He acted like a gentleman the entire time. Shortly after the walk ended, I handed him an honorarium check for his time on the road, and he handed it right back to me.

"It's for the cause, Gem," he said.

I was always in awe of my uncle. He personified

masculinity and everything I wanted to be. Even at sixty-seven, his biceps still popped out of his T-shirt when he'd roll up the awning outside the trailer. It's no wonder he beat cancer. My mother told me that when they were younger her girlfriends would line up by the fence on a hot day to look at him in the yard because his shirt was off. When he's not wearing a baseball cap, you can see he sports a tidy barbershop fade, and his thick wavy hair, the colour of gunmetal, is always combed nicely. He hunts and fishes. He fixes cars and works out four times a week.

Whenever he dropped me off at each leg on the highway, he'd watch me for a little while to make sure I was okay. Every now and then I'd look back and he'd still be standing there. It was a great comfort to me. I was reminded of the first time I ever rode a bike without training wheels. He unintentionally stole the glory from my mother, who took me around the neighbourhood every evening after she got off work to practice. One night when he was visiting, he asked to take me out instead.

"You don't need those training wheels anymore, Gem," he said.

"Are you sure, Uncle John?"

"I'll keep my hand on your back while you ride."

I was halfway down the street before I looked back and realized he let me go, though it felt like his hand was there, supporting me, the whole time.

You couldn't wipe the smile from my face. When I rode back to him, he picked me up and swung me around in the air. The bike had fallen on its side, but I didn't need it anymore because I felt like I was flying.

I ended the evening by doing an interview with Wendy Rose from *The Newfoundland Herald* as I soaked my feet in the warm bucket of water my uncle filled for me.

DAY 8

When I woke up the next day, the pain in my feet was unbearable. I hobbled around the trailer to get ready for the road. My mother had to help me get dressed because I had trouble balancing. I wrapped my feet in duct tape to give them more stability after I changed my bandages. It was pointless to try to squeeze my feet into sneakers because they were swollen. I decided to give my Crocs a try instead. As I was getting ready, a woman approached my uncle outside the trailer and asked to speak with me. She was the park manager and wanted to present me with a donation in person.

> Facebook Post: *"Day 8 began with a donation from the wonderful staff of Barachois Provincial Park for Pathways. We switch camps today. Corner Brook, you ready?"*

While I did my first interval, the team switched camps to Prince Edward Park in Corner Brook. I was experiencing more difficulty than usual as I walked and wasn't able to fully utilize each foot. I tried putting more pressure on the sides and rotating to the tips of my toes, but that caused my calves to cramp. The Crocs made walking somewhat tolerable, but I wasn't making any gains in terms of kilometers.

My walk was getting considerable media attention, and people were honking and waving at me as they passed. Many stopped to say hello. Joan Shea was one of those people. I was walking through her former district, and the hug I received from her that day gave me the boost I needed.

Facebook Post: "Nice visit from Joan Shea, former provincial politician, on the highway today!"

I became acquainted with Joan when she was in provincial politics as the Minister Responsible for the Status of Women. I was on the International Women's Day Planning Committee and the board of directors at the St. John's Status of Women Council. Each year, a group of us would meet with her at the Confederation Building to sign the proclamation for International Women's Day.

Later that day I noticed my legs were starting to swell. I decided to ignore it and continue on, but the inside of my thighs began to chafe due to the swelling. I had no other choice but to call it. There was no way I was going to be able to do the remaining two intervals. That meant I was now a full thirty-five kilometers behind my expected pace.

When I got back to the trailer, I noticed I had also broken out in hives. As I removed my bandages, I realized I had an allergic reaction to the glue in the duct tape. My feet looked so horrid that Justin insisted I go the hospital. I told my mother to hand me the Benadryl that I had packed and asked my uncle to run me an ice bath. I decided not to bandage my feet before bed that night and let them breathe. I placed a pillow between my legs where I was chafed, and when I slipped my feet beneath the covers they were so raw it was as if the cotton sheets had teeth. I fell asleep not long after, Al Pittman's selected poems in my arms.

Facebook Post: "Stephenville and neighbouring communities, you have my heart. Despite being covered in blisters and insect bites, you still got a smile out of me! I'm grateful for your donations, the invites into your homes, the stops along the highway and the stories you shared with me about how religious institutional abuse impacted this area. You're with me all the way! Wela'lin."

DAY 9

At 8:15 a.m. we made our way to the Grenfell Campus of Memorial University in Corner Brook. I had an interview scheduled with Gerri Lynn Mackey from CFCB at 8:30 a.m., and there was an event for me at 9:00 a.m. organized by a group of students and the City of Corner Brook. The room was full, and people were eager to speak to me following the event.

Facebook Post: "Day 9 begins with an interview with CFCB and an event at the Grenfell campus, then lots of walking!"

City Councilor Mary Ann Murphy brought greetings on behalf of the town and presented me with a donation. She invited me to say a few words. I talked about how encouraging it was to see so many young people at the event. I decided to remain on message instead of focusing on the toll the walk was taking on my body. On the inside, I was feeling disheartened and vulnerable, but on the outside I remained positive and strong.

When the event ended, I went to see a physiotherapist. Justin booked an appointment when my planter fasciitis and Achilles tendonitis began to flare a couple days after I started walking. The physiotherapist worked around the state of my feet, but he confirmed that it was possible to have a reaction to the glue on tapes and bandages. He applied hypoallergenic bandages to my feet when he finished. I went back to the campsite and ate my lunch and waited for a journalist from CBC.

> Facebook Post: "Just finished an interview with CBC's Colleen Connors airing tonight on Here and Now. A late start to walking means a 30k consecutive stretch in the hot sun."

Given the condition of my feet, I managed to squeeze in two intervals. As I walked, it started to sprinkle gently. The tiny drops of rain broke the heat. I was behind another ten kilometers.

Back at the trailer, my mother put the map of Newfoundland on the wall in my bedroom. She took out a marker and traced the distance I had already covered. The visual gave me hope and incentive.

"You love Newfoundland," she said. "And Newfoundland loves you."

DAY 10

After a solid sleep, I woke up feeling refreshed. The swelling in my feet and legs had decreased considerably, and the hives disappeared from my body. I got dressed, bandaged my feet, put on a pair of socks and slipped them gently into my hikers. I left the laces untied. My mother drove me to a meeting while my uncle went on a supply run with Justin.

*Facebook Post: "Day 10 begins having breakfast
with Archbishop Hundt and from there, another
long stretch of walking. I'm thankful for cool,
breezy weather today."*

Peter Hundt was the archbishop of the Diocese of Corner
Brook and Labrador. During our meeting, he told me that he
grew up on a farm in Ontario and entered the seminary after
high school. He was ordained at the age of twenty-six and
received a license in Canon Law five years later. His resume
was as comprehensive as it was impressive. He may have
been fifty-nine when we met, but the light grey hair carefully
combed above his forehead could easily be mistaken as
blonde. His glasses softened the distinct features of his
face. He was reserved, yet seemed to be secure in his own
skin. He wore his collar to our meeting and when I saw the
Birkenstocks on his feet, I joked that I had received my
license to become a lesbian when I bought my first pair of
Birks. I don't think he knew how to take me, but he sat across
from me for an hour. The fact that I was openly gay didn't
stop him from complimenting me on the work I was doing.
Perhaps I can work with this guy, I thought to myself.

Before the walk began I sent a letter to all the bishops in
the province to inform them of Hope Walk. I also invited
them to meet with me and make a donation. Bishop Hundt
and Archbishop Currie of St. John's were the only two
who responded. Bishop Hundt provided me with a personal
check for one hundred dollars since his diocese had gone
bankrupt due to sexual abuse claims. Archbishop Currie
provided a check from the archdiocese of St. John's for five
hundred dollars.

My mother took a picture of Bishop Hundt presenting me with his check in the parking lot of MacDonald's. After that, she drove me to the highway marker. Before I began to walk I called my friend, the good priest, to wish him a happy birthday. Hearing his voice perked me up. He told me I'd find a way through it all.

To my left was the magnificent Humber River. As I walked, I imagined its current carrying me. The beautiful mountains to my right also provided a needed lift. My load began to lighten. By the end of the day, I completed two intervals of twenty kilometers. I was still behind, but gaining momentum.

Facebook Post: "Corner Brook, how sweet are you at all! Not only did I get lots of honks, waves and hugs, I got a donation from the Archbishop and another from a Councilor on behalf of the City! Deer Lake, get ready!"

CONFESSION

I fell in love for the first time at the age of eight. She was two years my senior (no surprise to those who know me) and the prettiest girl in school. Her name was Tammy, and when she sang in the church choir, her voice lifted me so high it was as if I had wings. She lived with her family just down the street. Her house was shabby looking from the outside, and the car her father drove had been parked on the side of her house for months. It was rusty and the fender was almost off.

It only cost me a Mr. Freeze, one of those frozen juice pops in a plastic tube, to find out from her friend, Andrea, about the doll that Tammy wanted from Woolworth's, but couldn't afford. So I made it my mission to get it for her. I decided to risk everything for love, even my mortal soul. On Sundays, during Mass, my mother would hand me change from her purse for the collection plate, and I'd lower my hand into the basket just enough so that it looked like the change was being dropped inside. I'd pull my hand out carefully, fist full of coins, and steadily slip it into my pocket. After five consecutive Sundays, Tammy got her doll, and I got her attention.

Months later, I wasn't sure what to expect when I went with my class to the church for our First Confession. I remember asking my classmates what they were going to say. I knew we were required to say specific lines in response to the priest. We were given those lines in advance as homework. Our teacher told us to practice them until we knew them by heart. When the day arrived, I knew the script, but I was having a difficult time deciding what sins to tell the priest. I asked my friends what sins they were going to confess, so I could have a frame of reference. One boy told me he was going to make up some sins just to keep things interesting. But he was always getting into trouble at school, so I didn't understand why he'd have to make up anything at all. Another classmate said she was going to come clean about feeding her dog, Fluffy, the vegetables that her mother put on her plate at dinnertime. And someone else added that she was going to mention the time when she spoke out of turn in class and the teacher put her in the corner. *I must be really sinful*, I thought. I took the collection money my mother gave me to buy Tammy a doll. But God had to forgive me. After all, that's what God does for a living.

Then it was my turn to go in. The confessional was dark and the air was as heavy as the sin-burdened souls who entered there. I kneeled down and clasped my hands together tightly as if I was about to pray. When the priest opened the shutter and appeared behind the screen of the confessional, his face was turned from me. I was about to bare my heart and soul to him. The least he could do was look at me, I thought.

"Father, can you look at me?"

He seemed surprised by my request, but he did as I asked. He was a gentle, older priest and well liked among his parishioners. His face was as round as his dark-rimmed glasses. He was short, but his presence was uplifting. When he was assigned to another parish, we were all sad to see him go.

I made the sign of the cross and said, "Bless me, Father, for I have sinned."

But then I went off script again. I told the priest I learned the difference between mortal and venial sins in class, but I didn't know how to be sorry for my sin because I didn't know what type of sin it was.

At first he seemed rather confused, if not a little fascinated.

"What is your sin, my child," he asked.

"Mom handed me change for collection, and I kept it so I could buy something for a girl whose family is poor. And we have to help those less fortunate, right, Father?"

I swear I saw a grin come over the priest's face when I told him what I had done, but the confessional was so dimly lit I couldn't be sure. He invited me to offer an Act of Contrition, and so I recited what I had memorized:

"O my God, I am sorry for my sins with all my heart. In choosing to do wrong and failing to do good, I have sinned against You Whom I should love above all things. I firmly intend, with Your help, to do penance, to sin no more, and to avoid whatever leads me to sin. Our Saviour Jesus Christ suffered and died for us. In His name, my God, have mercy."

He told me that while my intentions were good and my cause was a noble one, I did take the money without permission. He advised me to do an act of charity for my mother. In the meantime, as my penance, he told me to say the Hail Mary three times. When I compared my penance to that of my classmates, I felt like I got off easy. So when I left school that day, I went home and I didn't just clean my room, I tidied the house, dusted the furniture, and vacuumed the carpet. When my grandfather saw how hard I was working, he slipped me a two-dollar bill and told me not to tell my mother. I asked him if he thought I should put it in collection on Sunday, and he told me that I'd done enough for one day. He made a compelling point. I smiled as I pocketed my crisp, pink two-dollar bill and waited enthusiastically for my mother to get home from work.

RESETTLEMENT

There's something eerie about visiting a resettled community in Newfoundland. Boards hang off the skeletal frames of houses like loose teeth, and the shadows of schools are imprinted upon the grassy knolls like ink pressed against a page in a history book. It was written, but perhaps it was foretold. Premier Joey Smallwood's spin on his government's resettlement plan resulted in the abandonment of three hundred communities. Despite the government's three attempts between 1954 and 1975 to consolidate the rural populations into major growth centres, the same social issues remain in the rural parts of the island and haunt the legislature to this very day.

Although I grew up in the province's capital city of St. John's and never experienced resettlement firsthand, I can imagine the pain those people must have felt as they left their homes, and I feel a certain kinship with them. I spent a lot of time living out of a suitcase as a child because my parents were divorced, and I went back and forth between two houses.

But I never felt at home in the other house I lived in—my body. I seemed to always move further away from myself. As far as I could go, never wanting to leave, but not knowing how to stay. It was as if I was somehow displaced. No matter where I went, it was as though I was living somewhere else. As if I'd been towing my body behind me all my life. When I tried to move forward, it held me back to the point that I never really felt at home within myself. I tried to resettle and settle for less than what I was. But it was all based on a lie similar to the one Smallwood told—this way will be better for everyone.

– – – – –

I was a child when I met him. I worshipped him like a god, but not just because he was a priest. He paid attention to me. I felt special. I went to mass every day, sometimes twice. I came from a long line of devout Roman Catholics. Faith seemed the only constant in my life at that time, besides him. He took me under his wing, and I felt safe and sheltered. He took me places. Bought me things. I thought he did all of that because he cared. I was wrong. It was called *grooming*.

After we'd known one another for some time, he invited me over for supper at the rectory. When he pulled a plate out of the fridge, I thought it odd that his housekeeper only put enough food away for one person. *Didn't he tell her I was coming?* I wondered. He took another plate out of the cupboard and gave me one of the small pork chops. He cut the baked potato in half and separated the green peas equally between the two plates. We sat at the dining-room table—he at the helm and I to his left. I brought up the books I was reading. I enjoyed discussing theology.

"You're brighter than most, Gemma," he said as he squeezed my arm with his hand. Once we finished eating, he suggested we move to the couch. He offered me some wine even though I wasn't old enough to drink. But that wasn't uncommon for him. Whenever he performed a wedding in my family, he would save his drink tickets for my younger cousins and me. We all thought God would forgive us for drinking under age because a priest gave us the drink tickets. He made me feel special. Though I wouldn't feel that way much longer.

– – – – –

"Oh Jesus," he cried out. But he was far from praying. His body shook as it emptied; the cross that hung from around his neck knocked against my chin to the rhythm of his jerking body as he loomed above me. He shouted "Jesus" two more times as he finished. When he was done, he got up from the couch, his penis still leaking. It soaked the front part of his light-blue cotton boxers and reeked like bleach and sour milk. I got up slowly and staggered down the hallway. On my way to the washroom, I saw a picture of Jesus pointing at his Sacred Heart. I wanted to point towards my heart, too. I grew up seeing images like that of Jesus, but in that moment I felt like my heart was pierced and wrapped in a ring of thorns.

I shut the door and locked it. I could barely stand to look at myself in the mirror. I felt so much shame as I hovered over the sink. I quickly splashed some water over me. My entire body felt like a gaping wound. I wondered if it would ever close. Even after cleaning myself, I still felt dirty, forever stained by the scar of his sin. *Perhaps Jesus does save*, I thought, because fixating on the cross around his neck took my mind away from what was actually happening.

When I came out of the washroom, he was waiting for me at the top of the stairs that led to the vestibule. He reached for his jacket and ascot hat.

"If you stay here any longer, I'd want to have intercourse upstairs," he said. "I'm going to take you home now."

Was that supposed to make me feel better? He liked me so much that he would like to rape me on his bed?

For a long time after, I'd wake up with night sweats. I'd have dreams of him looking at me from the altar with piercing eyes. Every now and then, I'd see him out somewhere and it would haunt me for days. Once I bumped into him at the grocery store. He was standing over the dairy section. I put the carton of eggs down and started walking in the other direction. I had to force myself to leave my house every day for a week after that.

Years later, when my godfather passed away, the priest actually showed up at the funeral home. It's a good thing my mother wasn't in the room at the time. She had stepped out to pick up more food. My stepfather tried to warn me, but I didn't realize it because I was in the middle of speaking with a friend. But when I turned around, there he was. And there I was standing in front of my godfather's coffin with no other choice but to confront the loss of two father figures all at once. The grief outweighed the anger, and I didn't want to make a scene. He put out his arms and I opened mine. When we embraced, he told me he was sorry, and I told him that I forgave him. No one else knew what had just transpired.

"I see you in the news all the time," he said as he started to cry.

At that moment, I realized he wasn't the scary monster that I had to fear anymore. He was human and weak like the rest of us. But the difference with me was that I was getting stronger. I wasn't the vulnerable one now.

"I didn't like how it all went down," I told him.

Truthfully, all I wanted from him was an apology. But neither my parents nor my lawyer seemed to think it was a good idea. No one understood how hard I struggled with losing him, or rather losing the idea of him. It impacted my entire worldview because of how much I looked up to him. I didn't want money. I wanted peace. But the choices were either go to court or settle outside of court. My lawyer wanted to spare me the trial. The priest's lawyer wanted his client's reputation to remain intact. But signing a confidentiality agreement made it worse. The secrecy in my life was crippling. My father was hiding his alcohol addiction. I was hiding my sexuality. And now I was hiding the fact that I was abused. And all of this concealment and deception could be traced back to the Catholic Church and the culture of secrecy, which created an atmosphere of dependency and shame.

— — — — —

My lawyer's office was located on Church Hill, directly across from the Anglican Cathedral's oldest cemetery. The big bay window in his third-floor office framed the ancient trees that jutted upwards, their leaves exploding like green fireworks into the sky above the street below. Too painful in the moment, my eyes focused on those trees as my lawyer transcribed, word for word, everything I said. He and my stepfather were good friends, so he agreed to represent me against the priest and the archdiocese.

"The fact that you remember the way the priest said 'Jesus' three times is helpful," he noted as he proceeded to read a section of the statement back to me.

The shame engulfed me like a wildfire, snuffed out moments later with tears. I needed a release. Much like those nameless bodies submerged under endless layers of gravel on the opposite side of the street, I buried this secret deep within me, hoping it would never surface. Now that I was forced to dig it up, I didn't feel any lighter.

The lawyer jumped up from his desk to retrieve a box of tissues from the mantle, and as he handed them to me, our eyes locked. I felt safe within the confines of his gentle gaze. As a lawyer, he was focused on the facts, but when he saw I was slipping, his humanity brought me back. We had to finish what we started in order to move forward. I wiped my eyes and picked up where we left off.

As I got older I was haunted by what happened. It followed me into my relationships. I didn't trust anyone. I felt like it was my fault. The guilt was eating me up inside. I confided in another priest, one I felt comfortable talking to as we had developed a friendship. He encouraged me to tell my parents and agreed to be in the room with me when I did. That's why I refer to him as "the good priest." He held my hand to stop me from shaking. The next day, he contacted the archbishop. My parents hired a lawyer, and I met with the church's liaison in my lawyer's office to give him my statement. I cried the entire time. The process itself took years. I knew of one other victim that had been assaulted by this priest, but she didn't want to come forward. So in order to ensure he wouldn't be in a position to harm anyone else, I insisted he retire early. I received a cash settlement from him, and the church committed to paying a therapist to treat me for the rest of my life. The priest admitted to what had happened to the church's liaison, though he was never charged. He maintained his reputation because I signed a confidentiality agreement, which my lawyer said would give me closure so I could move on with my life. End of story, right? Not quite.

Flash forward to two decades later. I took out a loan and went back to university to complete the undergraduate degree that I attempted to sabotage years before. I had just received a medal for my contribution to gay rights in Canada, and I got a great job running a center that offers art education to at-risk youth. I was doing okay.

But that quickly changed when I was forced to speak with the archbishop's assistant on the phone. She insisted I go see my lawyer and get a copy of the settlement agreement so the church could verify whether or not they were still required to pay for my therapy. And because the files were no longer at the diocese, they didn't know what priest sexually assaulted me.

Unbelievably, the priest who sexually assaulted me came out of retirement and was placed in charge of two churches. I was furious. That conversation, and the ones that followed, unsealed a deep wound. I experienced depression and anxiety regularly and had to go on anti-depressants. At times, my entire body was flooded with anger. I worried that the anger would boil over and seep into every aspect of my life.

So I committed to working through my feelings with my therapist, and when I found healthy ways to cope with my depression and anxiety, eventually the anger began to fade away. But if I was dealing with all of these things, I couldn't imagine what others were going through, especially if they didn't have access to the same resources and supports as I did thanks to my privilege and public profile. Now I had an idea to create a new organization, but as an experienced worker within the non-profit sector, I knew it would have to be sustainable, so I did my research. I conducted key-stakeholder interviews with lawyers who represented survivors, as well as survivors and their family members. I conducted focus groups with community organizations, government departments, and even religious groups. I sought out appropriate board members with expertise in areas such as restorative justice, academia, communications, and law. And in December of 2013, I incorporated the Pathways Foundation.

I was finished with resettling and decided it was time to rebuild.

HOPE WALK:
DEER LAKE TO SOUTH BROOK

DAY 12

The last few days on the highway had rocked me to my core. The rain tumbled like hail from the sky, and the howl of the wind would cause even a wolf to startle. I dug in enough to withstand the wind on the outside, but on the inside I felt shaken. I still had miles to go, and that distance had less to do with the highway and more to do with me understanding myself. I realized it wasn't just my sexuality I was struggling with all these years, but my gender also. And though I've spent many years in therapy working through the abuse I endured, I was still hurting. Hearing stories from other clergy abuse survivors who stopped to talk to me on the road caused my fury to swell—I felt a storm brewing within.

But when I arrived in Deer Lake, the glint from the sun made it seem as though the sky was smiling. I decided to veer off course and followed a path that led to a lake.

Facebook Post: "Yesterday the rain was harsh and unrelenting and the howl of the wind was fierce, but I walked steady through it and today, on Day 12, a calm came from within. I lay down on a beach in Deer Lake under a sky of clouded blue."

I never knew Deer Lake had a beach. I only ever passed through the town by car, and I don't even think I stopped at a gas station to use the washroom or fill up. Clearly I had been missing out. Walking across the island gave me the opportunity to visit places I'd never been before. And having just walked through the worst kind of weather, while dealing with a tremendous amount of inner turmoil, I felt renewed by the sun's light. No matter the storm, blue skies are never far behind.

Walls of lanky grass concealed a lakeside shoreline swathed with sand and pebbles. I took off my sneakers and socks and sat down close to the water's edge because it was so clear and inviting. My feet looked like two giant red grapes because of the discolouration. They were still extremely tender, but the gentle breeze nudged the cool water to rush over them in small waves, making them feel refreshed. I was adamant about wrapping them in bandages, using compression to stem the swelling, but letting them breathe the night before seemed to make a difference. I took a tube of Vaseline from my pocket, pulled up my shorts, and rubbed some into my inner thighs. The petroleum jelly took the edge off the chafing, especially when I walked.

I unzipped my backpack in search of my book of Robert Frost's poems and leaned back on an old log that was beached behind me. I was in the middle of reading "The Road

Not Taken" when a greyish-white straggly mutt, who thought I was worth a sniff, interrupted me. A few seconds later, an elderly woman stumbled trying to retrieve him. I jumped up and offered her my hand.

"So sorry for not seeing you there," she said. "I never let Rex off lead when there's people around."

"I'm the one who should be apologizing to Rex," I said. "I can't imagine my odor is very pleasing today."

The crown of her beige Tilley hat loosely lay on a bed of thick grey curls. It moved slightly as she laughed, forcing its brim to seep over the top of her retro, squared, tortoise-shell sunglasses. Once we were at eye level with each other, her laughter ceased.

"I believe I've seen you on television," she said.

"My name's Gemma," I responded, offering her my hand. "Rex and I are lucky to have such a fine day for our walks."

She hesitantly took my hand, but her words met me without reservation.

"I've never met a gay person before," she said.

"I'm sure you've met a gay person, but just didn't know it," I stressed.

In that suddenly awkward moment, I couldn't tell where our exchange was headed. Her manner was abrupt, but I didn't find her presence at all threatening. Our discussion was cut short when she unexpectedly became faint. She told me she had been walking her dog for some time before he decided to run off and that she was feeling dehydrated. I invited her to sit on the log and offered her a bottle of Gatorade from my backpack.

I couldn't be certain yet, but I felt she was a person of deep religious faith.

My undergraduate studies were mainly in comparative religions as I examined traditions in both the East and West. Looking at religions through a purely academic lens opened my eyes (and mind) and provided me with a new perspective on Catholicism—the faith I grew up in. Before I studied other religions, I had a blind faith when it came to my own. I had so many questions, and they eventually led me to a greater understanding of the world and the people in it. I credit my father for instilling in me an insatiable hunger for knowledge. Both my parents read to me as a child and encouraged me to read every day once I learned how to do it on my own, which I did constantly thereafter. But it was my father's library that fed me. The church may have placed the idea of God in my head, but in my father's book collection, I felt as though God was tangible. Books took me places, including out of my home when I needed to leave and physically couldn't. In my imagination, I slayed dragons—practice for the real life ones I hadn't yet figured out how to slay. There were no limits in literature, unlike in real life.

When I took courses that focused on Biblical languages, I was offered an alternate route to reading scripture and other religious texts. I enjoyed switching from Taoist texts to the Apocrypha, just to name a couple. I also found another way to understand my culture, and the island I grew up on, by taking courses in Religion in Newfoundland and Labrador with Dr. Hans Rollman. I remember discussing the Salvation Army and Pentecostals in Newfoundland with him, and how after they came to the island in the late nineteenth and early twentieth centuries, they settled in rural areas, mainly central and western industrialized towns because the social needs of the population increased. Deer Lake was one of those towns.

Before I joined her on the log, I cupped some lake water in the palm of my hand and offered it to Rex who was panting as he lay at her feet. He gave my hand a few licks, and I wiped his little brow with the rest. I could tell by her smile that the tiny gesture endeared me to her, so I struck up a conversation.

"I read somewhere that the Europeans who settled here called the caribou *deer* and that's how the town got its name," I said.

"Mainlanders," she said, as she playfully rolled her eyes before taking another mouthful of Gatorade.

In that moment, it occurred to me that, just like the categorizations we assign to gender, the names we collectively assign to others, even the ones we might think are harmless, like "mainlanders," are often too general, too fearful, and don't always reflect actualities or our best intentions.

"I'm all about new people coming to the island," I responded, "but those colonists messed some things up for sure."

We talked for a while longer. She told me that when the airport was built in 1955, it kept a lot of people in the town because they didn't have to seek work elsewhere.

"It's hard to be away from home," she said. "And working away from your family makes it even harder."

When she spoke, I recalled a joke I once heard: when Newfoundlanders die, we're the only ones who want to leave heaven because we're homesick for Newfoundland.

"Give me a swig of that, will ya?" I asked in a playful tone. "I'm parched."

She offered the Gatorade back to me without hesitation. When we finished the rest of the bottle, I told her I had to get a move on. She reached into her pocket, pulled out a twenty-dollar bill, and offered it as a donation.

"Well, Gemma, you weren't what I expected," she admitted.

"Honestly, these days, I even surprise myself," I told her.

During our discussion, my initial intuition was confirmed when she told me she was raised Pentecostal. I don't think her views changed completely because of our brief encounter, but the way she responded to me certainly did. When I offered her my hand to shake before we parted, she extended her arms instead. After we embraced, I reached down and patted Rex's little head. She wished me the best of luck. I thanked her and set out on the highway.

Back on the road, I felt pleased with that encounter. I felt I had made some small contribution, some small inroad, and the experience reminded me of Maude Barlow.

Maude is the Honorary Chairperson of the Council of Canadians and the co-founder of the Blue Planet Project. As an activist, she's always been an inspiration to me. Her efforts to raise awareness on the global water crisis have not only shifted the way many people think about purchasing bottled water, they've also changed public policy. She has published and contributed to countless books, won numerous awards, and has given talks all over the world, including one in St. John's in 2006, where she and I first met.

Through Maude, I learned that water covers seventy-one percent of the earth's surface. Most of it contains salt because it comes from the oceans. The remainder is fresh, but it makes up a very small percentage. Of that fresh water, most of it is ice. Water—clear, fresh, fluid, life-sustaining water—is precious. Yet major corporations regulate the majority of that fresh water. I believe access to clean, potable water is a human right. And thanks to Maude, the fearless water warrior, more people in other parts of the world believe that, too.

It wasn't the lake or all its fresh water that generated a memory of Maude; it was my encounter with the woman.

During my term as President of Egale Canada, the country's leading LGBTQ2+ advocacy organization since 1986, in addition to chairing monthly board meetings with representatives from different regions in Canada, I'd facilitate an annual retreat in Ottawa, where our offices were originally located. It provided the board and staff with the opportunity to connect in person and set our priorities for the coming year. Each year, we'd invite a guest speaker to address our board, and because one of our board members worked at the Council of Canadians, we were able to secure the legendary Maude Barlow.

Maude and I ended up chatting once she concluded her talk. She asked me if I'd be up for a visit to the REAL Women of Canada office located in the same building on the floor below. Formed in 1983, REAL stands for Realistic, Equal, Active for Life, and the group advocates for traditional marriage and 'family' values. They actively lobbied against same-sex marriage, while we, their neighbours, lobbied for it. So of course, when Maude, who in my opinion is one of the greatest activists of our time, invited me to join her, I was thrilled. I could feel the rush of adrenaline as I walked beside her, completely awestruck by her gentle yet mighty presence. When we arrived at their office, Maude softly knocked on the door. An elderly woman, who Maude knew by name, greeted us.

"This is my friend, Gemma," Maude told her. "Gemma is a charming Newfoundlander who I'm sure would love a cup of tea."

It was the best cup of tea I ever had. My paternal grand-mother always insisted that tea tastes better in a china teacup, but honestly I savoured every sip from a scratched up old coffee mug that day. I learned so much from watching the pleasant and peaceful exchange between those two incredible women. They put politics aside and talked about their everyday lives. It dawned on me that when two people start shouting, both parties stop listening. I've never been afraid of conflict, but the interaction between those two women, despite differences of opinion, made me rethink my approach when it came to activism.

After we left, Maude turned to me and said, "Gemma, never forget the power of your presence or how far a conversation can take you."

I never forgot that.

DAY 13

It was a mental game now. The emptiness of the highway and the distance I had left had nothing to do with it anymore. I was playing against myself. I pushed beyond not only the physical pain and the weather, but my doubts and fears as well. I was determined to win.

People took care of me on the road. They'd often pull over to get a picture and hand me a snack or a bottle of Gatorade.

Many of them revealed their deepest, darkest secrets to me and even let me hold them as they cried. All of their stories connected to the same narrative—a priest, brother, or nun abused them or a family member.

There was no confessional in the world big enough to hold what I heard. The stories were easier to carry while I was moving. But when I lay still in my bed at night, they haunted my dreams.

One woman, who was driving home from the mainland with her daughter for a visit, told me nuns abused her at Belvedere Orphanage in St. John's. Even though she had been living in Ontario for some time, I could still hear her Newfoundland accent.

"My darling, you got some face on you," she said. "Right handsome."

I loved it when a woman called me handsome. I felt like I was actually seen.

"Music and Friends," by the Newfoundland folk duo Simani, was playing in the background on the car stereo.

"I dies for that song," I told her.

"Makes me right homesick," she replied.

"Let's have a dance, sure, myself and you," I said, as I playfully winked at her daughter.

Within two seconds, she was out of the car and in my arms. We kicked up the dust as we sang out our lungs, waltzing on the dirt shoulder of the Trans-Canada Highway.

These light moments eclipsed the dark ones.

DAY 14

After my uncle dropped me off on the highway, my team

switched camps from Sir Richard Squires Memorial Park on the Humber River to George Huxter Memorial Park in Springdale.

I changed my walking pattern from three intervals of ten kilometers to two intervals of fifteen based on my energy level and pace.

The sun's light stretched across the sky as if it had wings. The entire landscape was aglow and so was I. Well rested, the splendor of my surroundings made the heat tolerable, as did a tiny brook that I immersed myself in during a short break.

> *Facebook Post: "Day 13 was hot and Day 14, even hotter. I found relief in a tumbling brook to cool my face and feet. The sky is the limit!"*

As I was walking, a silver sedan pulled over just ahead of me on the other side of the road. Two small boys jumped out and attempted to run across the highway until an elderly woman got out of the vehicle and grabbed them both by the hand. The boys started to jump up and down as they waved at me. I motioned to the woman to stay put, checked both directions, and jogged (more like hobbled quickly) across the road to meet them.

The woman greeted me with a big hug. Her husband, who was driving, exited the vehicle and came over to say hello. He shook my hand with what seemed like reverence. She introduced herself and her two grandsons. She told me that they live in Nova Scotia, but are originally from Newfoundland. They wanted to come back for a visit and decided to take their two grandsons along to show them the island. They heard about my walk on the radio, and were hoping to meet me. She herself had been abused and wanted to get a picture with me. One of the boys ran back to the vehicle to retrieve a small Newfoundland flag. He waved it softly over my head as if I'd already crossed the finish line. I welcomed the slight breeze.

"Captain Newfoundland," he declared.

Her husband took out his phone to take a picture. While we posed, her grandson held the flag in the opposite direction. *Captain Newfoundland with a queer twist*, I chuckled to myself and wondered if Geoff Stirling—the Newfoundland media mogul who owned Newfoundland Television (NTV) and the magazine *The Newfoundland Herald*—would see the irony, too.

The boy was too young to know of the Captain New-foundland comic strip from *The Newfoundland Herald* or the movie that aired on NTV in the late seventies called, *Captain Newfoundland and the Tip of Atlantis*, but I never forgot the captain's code, and years later I discovered how much it resembled a line from Shakespeare: "This above all: to thine own self be true."

DAY 15

When I got out of bed I looked at the Newfoundland map on the wall in the trailer and traced my finger along the ink trail to the middle, where it ended. I gave the map a knowing nod. I reached my halfway mark. In my mind I was already home.

The smell of bacon frying lured me into the kitchen. John and Justin were seated at the dinette. My mother was at the stove making breakfast. Whenever it was time to switch camps we would regroup over a big breakfast of bacon, eggs, beans and toast and wash it all down with a cup of Tetley in true Newfoundland fashion.

Both sets of my grandparents performed the ritual of table dining at every single meal. Neither one of my grandmother's would approve of the dishes we were using on the road or the fact that there wasn't a tablecloth. I can still hear the snap of the freshly pressed linen as it was being cast through the air before it caught the end of the table. The old ways seem to be lost on my generation, but an amazing poet, whom I'd grown to care for deeply, taught me to appreciate the art of dining again.

For my first interval, two friends joined me: Philip Alcock, who was one of my trainers for the walk, and Dr. Jennifer Lokash, the Department Head of English at Memorial University. They met me at the campsite shortly after we finished breakfast. Phil hoisted me in his arms when he saw me and planked me down on the picnic table in front of the trailer. He stretched my legs and gave me a much-needed back massage. After he finished, he put me on his back and carried me to the truck. At six foot five and weighing 275 pounds of muscle, Phil is a gentle giant.

Having company on the road lifted my mood. In addition to the two friends cheering me on, I was receiving thousands of encouraging messages from people all over the province, and from people in Ontario and Alberta now too. Thanks to the great Newfoundland diaspora, news of my walk was spreading across the country.

Refreshed and refocused, I finished both intervals without issue and ended the day at the entrance of our new campsite—Kona Beach Park.

WELL JUNG

Her hair was the colour of coal. It formed the shape of a pyramid and framed her pale white face. I focused my attention elsewhere whenever she looked directly at me. But when her head was lowered to jot down notes, I studied her closely, so much so I could even see the tiny strands of grey hairs that hovered above her head like ash. Her black-rimmed glasses were goggle-like. I wondered if she could see that I was drowning. We sat in two upholstered chairs directly opposing one another. Between us was an oval table that had a small potted fern, a box of tissues, and an alarm clock on top. The clock ticked obtrusively as if a bomb were about to go off. My head hung as if my neck had been snapped. It took me approximately forty-five minutes to utter the words, and when she reminded me that there were only fifteen minutes remaining, I blurted it out. Life, as I knew it, exploded.

"I like girls, and my doctor told me there's no cure for it," I confessed.

Up until that moment, I had only told my family doctor. I tried desperately to keep it hidden. But everything changed, at the age of fifteen, when I spent the night with a girl.

"I dare you to kiss me on my stomach, Gemma," she tempted. And so our encounter progressed almost as a dare. We had similar bodies, but I never wanted mine in the same way I wanted hers.

We barely spoke after that night. Lying with her felt like a dream, but my reality became a living nightmare. The hatred I felt for myself amplified as the questions raced through my mind. Would she tell people? Would I have to go to another high school? Would I be kicked out of my house? Would God forgive me? When I told my family doctor what was wrong with me he referred me to a therapist.

"I'm here to help you," the therapist said. "And so is God."

I could tell by the type of crucifix she was wearing that she was Catholic. It hung from her neck on a long dark string, and as she sat upright in the chair, its base tunnelled into her white cotton blouse.

"I base my approach on Carl Jung," she specified. "Homosexuality is pre-mature, but the good news is that, with treatment, you'll come into full sexual maturity once you become heterosexual."

I was well-read for my age, so I had heard of Jung, but I always thought he and Freud were lovers because they wrote letters to one another.

"Your attraction to other girls is rooted in your desire to be more like them," she stated, her tone detached.

In my mind, I disagreed with her analysis. I never wanted to be like a "girl" because even though I was assigned female at birth I never felt like one. As she adjusted her glasses for the third time, I felt like a specimen under a microscope. According to her, it was possible for me to become a heterosexual through quiet reflection and prayer. At the time, I was so desperate to change I would've believed whatever she said. She prescribed some books to read and gave me advice on how to improve my method of prayer. I did as she instructed. She was the expert after all. When nothing worked, I made the decision to end my life.

APPLES AND ORANGES

"Count backwards from one hundred," the doctor said.

"I can't even do that when I'm sober."

She laughed. Humour was my defense. Shortly after, I was moved out of Emergency to the psychiatric ward.

I was sixteen years old; my last year of high school was just beginning. I was a good student and popular among my friends, so when word got around that I had attempted suicide, people were shocked.

I wanted to be dead because I hated myself. I didn't think twice about it. I drank a flask of rum and swallowed a bottle of pills as if they were medicine—as if they could cure my "disease." Death must be better than living as a gay person, I told myself.

Before my suicide attempt, I tried not to be gay. When I found myself feeling something for another girl, I took a cold bath or had sex with my boyfriend, even though it was starting to feel dishonest. I went to church each day and prayed to God at night. I read every book I could find on reparative therapy and even attended sessions with a conversion therapist. When nothing worked, I wrote a good-bye note to my parents and put a plan in place.

Spending a few weeks on the psychiatric ward gave me a chance to clear my head. I became friends with another patient who was a gay man. He took me under his wing. I also met a nurse who was gay, and she was very kind. All of a sudden, gay people didn't seem so bad, and I didn't feel alone.

The other patients were friendly, too. Because I was much younger, they showed me the ropes. They pointed out the nurses who let patients sleep in and told me the doctors to avoid. Fortunately, the one assigned to me wasn't on their list.

After a few sessions, I finally told the psychiatrist that I had tried to take my own life because I was gay. His response surprised me: he told me that homosexuality hadn't been considered a mental illness since the early 1970s.

"Where do you think all this hate comes from?" he asked.

"I was raised Roman Catholic, Doc, and spoon-fed Irish ballads as a baby. I thought being gay was a sin, and every song I ever heard my uncle sing was about the love between a man and a woman," I answered.

"It's no wonder you're in here," he said. "Irish ballads can do that to a person. There's nothing wrong with you. I'm sending you home."

He must be a Protestant, I thought.

After I left hospital, I gradually "came out" and realized I had internalized my homophobia. No one kicked me out of my house or disowned me. No one beat me up or called me names or refused to be my friend like some gay people experience. I was one of the lucky ones.

My mother cried when I told her, but not because she was sad. She told me she had seen stories on the news about gay people being beaten, even killed, and she didn't want that to happen to her child. She wanted me to live a full life.

"You won't be able to get married now," she said, tears streaming down her face. "I kept my wedding dress for you."

"It's okay, Mom," I said. "I don't like wearing dresses anyway."

Almost a decade later, much had changed. In 2003, I was on a plane to Halifax to present a brief on same-sex marriage on behalf of the Lesbian, Bi-sexual, Gay, Transgender (LBGT-MUN) resource centre I ran while attending Memorial University. At that time, the issue was a hot topic of debate, so the federal government formed a Standing Committee on Justice and Human Rights that travelled to every province (with the exception of Newfoundland and Labrador) and invited organizations to present position papers, both for and against.

The lobby of the Casino Nova Scotia Hotel was filled with protesters. I waded through them cautiously, as if walking in thick brush. I couldn't see their faces because they held their signs up high. But one man didn't have a sign. I'll always remember his face because he spit in mine. I eyed him while I wiped my face with my sleeve and made my way to the salon, trying not to appear shaken by what just happened.

The room was large with no windows and packed with people. Some were parents who brought their children; some were pastors who brought their flocks. One translator lined the back wall with her equipment, and six politicians sat at a table in front of her. We activists sat in the middle of it all, not knowing what to expect.

37th PARLIAMENT, 2nd SESSION
Standing Committee on Justice and Human Rights
Monday, April 7, 2003
Halifax, Nova Scotia

Growing up is not easy, for many reasons, but even more so for lesbian and gay youth. As a youth, I often felt alienated from the world around me. When I became an adolescent, this feeling continued, until I embraced my sexuality and acknowledged it openly. Thankfully, my family and friends were very accepting. Unfortunately, many lesbians and gays do not have the same experience, because of the lack of societal recognition. This lack of recognition extends to our relationships, which, from personal experience, I can say are as significant as heterosexual relationships.

Such societal indifference has profoundly negative consequences for lesbians and gays on many levels. Therefore, the status quo is completely unacceptable. Some form of legally recognized separate, but equal relationship segregation is completely unacceptable. Further delay in the official recognition of the rights of lesbian and gay relationships is also completely unacceptable. The only viable and moral option is to extend the legal definition of marriage to treat same-sex and opposite-sex couples equally.

It is not a secret that the major argument against same-sex marriage in Canada comes from the conservative elements of Christianity, who, whether they argue against lesbian and gay rights on explicitly religious grounds, argue fundamentally from a sense of feeling. As a Christian, I understand the conflict other Christians experience in attempting to reconcile the apparent teachings of Christianity with the rapid evolution of the modern world. I also have compassion for those who are afraid for the fate of their treasured social institutions during these times of change. However, I believe it is unequivocal that these fears, in the case of same-sex marriage, are groundless, and legal recognition of same-sex marriage will be a positive change.

I suspect that even the Christian Church will soon be ready to come to terms with the full acceptance of same-sex marriage, as it has adapted to many changes in the past. That being said, this is Canada. And Canada is a secular country, where all Canadian citizens are free to practice or not practice any religion as they see fit, as long as it does not infringe on the rights of others. Unfortunately, respecting, on a legal level, Christian beliefs that discriminate against lesbians and gays infringes the inalienable rights of all Canadians, especially Canadians of a minority sexual orientation. Therefore, religious arguments against same-sex marriage are not acceptable in this debate.

I will now briefly address the three most dismissible arguments against same-sex marriage:

First, there is no conceivable way same-sex marriage could cheapen existing marriages, damage the institution of marriage or, in extreme cases, contribute to the already high divorce rate in heterosexual marriages or influence heterosexuals not to marry at all. If fairness to lesbians and gays could produce such deleterious results, we must ask ourselves how meaningful the institution of marriage is in the first place. The opponents of same-sex marriage present this unlikely scenario without offering any concrete evidence to support it. Truthfully, no such evidence exists, because the notion is preposterous to begin with and rooted in ignorance rather than common sense.

Second, it is often argued that lesbians and gays do not have monogamous relationships. This is a slanderous falsehood. Many lesbians and gays demonstrably do have monogamous relationships. If there also exist many lesbians and gays who are not in monogamous relationships, just as there exist many heterosexuals who are not in monogamous relationships, this cannot possibly serve as a justification to deny the rights of those who are. If some argue that not being in monogamous relationships is bad and that the institution of marriage encourages monogamous relationships, surely, extending marriage to lesbians and gays will alleviate this problem. Denying marriage to lesbians and gays exacerbates the problem and has a direct and negative impact on a lot of lesbian and gay Canadians and on Canadian society as a whole.

Third, some opponents of same-sex marriage contend that marriage is an institution uniquely constituted for the purposes of promoting and nurturing procreation and that since lesbians and gays supposedly cannot procreate, which is not true, as we are quite capable of procreation through the intervention of a third party, just like infertile heterosexual couples, it does not make sense to extend marriage to this group. This argument is risible on many levels. Marriage is a contractual arrangement that confers many rights and obligations that have been tuned over time to serve the real needs of couples, but nowhere in Canadian law does it specify that married couples must procreate. If some opponents of same-sex marriage want to be consistent, they should lobby to forbid infertile and post-menopausal women the right to marry and for the annulment of marriages that do not produce offspring by some deadline.

In reading material on the subject of this committee written by some of my honourable Presbyterian colleagues, I have noted the suggestion that they and other Canadian groups would like to have more time to study this issue. It is hard not to respect the desire to thoroughly examine this issue before making what must seem like a major change *to the structure of Canadian law as it relates to such a fundamental institution. Nevertheless, I believe this issue has been studied and talked about enough and now is the time to act.*

I respect the rights of all churches to sanction or not sanction homosexuality and homosexual relationships as they see fit, but in Canada we have freedom of religion, and that necessarily means freedom from religion. The values of our society are changing, and we have reached a point where the notion of same-sex marriage has achieved a high level of mainstream acceptance. That, coupled with the very important points that marriage is an issue with direct, here and now, bread and butter importance to many Canadian couples who are currently denied that right and that marriage for lesbians and gays is a matter of fundamental justice and equal rights, indicates very strongly that society cannot wait any longer to move decisively on this issue. Justice delayed is justice denied. It may be a cliché, but it is no doubt a timeless truth.

Thank you for your time and consideration.

After I delivered my brief, I felt empowered. I left the room and searched the lobby for the man who spit on me, but he was gone. I wanted to thank him for what he had done, because being degraded in such a public way had influenced how I presented my brief that day. It had also inspired me to dedicate the next two decades of my life to the gay-rights movement, and to same-sex marriage specifically.

As a feminist, I had struggled with the historical implications of the concepts behind "marriage." Ultimately for me, feminism means having the freedom to choose, and if some same-sex couples wished to marry, they should have that option.

After returning to St. John's, I became involved with Newfoundland Gays and Lesbians for Equality (NGALE) and soon was elected co-chair. I joined the St. John's Pride Committee and formed a chapter of Parents and Friends of Lesbians and Gays (PFLAG) in St. John's. I also developed an outreach project for Planned Parenthood Newfoundland and Labrador that coached doctors, nurses, social workers, teachers, youth care workers, and clergy on how to offer support to LGBTQ2+ youth. It was the first project of its kind in the province.

My work locally was getting attention nationally, and I was encouraged by other gay activists to run for the position of Atlantic Rep with Egale Canada. Not long after I was elected, I became president of that national organization and was appointed to the executive of a newly formed group called Canadians for Equal Marriage. Working side-by-side with activists from all across Canada made me feel less alienated. Geographically, Newfoundland and Labrador is separated from the rest of Canada. Growing up on an island can be isolating, especially when you're gay and closeted.

By 2004, same-sex marriage was legal in seven provinces. Newfoundland and Labrador wasn't one of them. But I knew that many same-sex couples in my home province wanted to get married. I proposed orchestrating a court case in Newfoundland and Labrador to my colleagues at Canadians for Equal Marriage and Egale Canada.

My next step was to recruit same-sex couples to be involved in a court case. A month later, I found two lesbian couples who were willing to go public. Both couples had been together for many years and wanted to get married. I brought them to Vital Statistics to apply for marriage licenses, and they were denied.

I called a lawyer from Nova Scotia who had represented same-sex couples in a similar court case there, to take on this case. Once he agreed, he filed suit against both the provincial and federal governments on behalf of the couples.

When our court date arrived, I met with the two couples in the courtroom to debrief before the proceedings began. The walls were covered in stained oak from top to bottom. Large windows hung from the wall like paintings in an art gallery.

There were long oak benches lined up like church pews in the back. I sat in the first row with the two couples. The lawyers were ahead of us, in a separate section, closer to the judge: the lawyer for the two couples, the lawyer for the Attorney General of Newfoundland and Labrador, and the lawyer for the Attorney General of Canada.

The judge granted limited intervener status to a pastor; he was up front, as well. The public were also allowed to be in the courtroom. Behind us on one side were activists and family members of the two couples. On the opposing side were members of the pastor's congregation.

The judge that presided over the case seemed so thorough I doubted there would be grounds for appeal from either side.

"This isn't going to be a rubber-stamp courtroom," he warned.

After the lawyers spoke and informed the judge they would not oppose, the pastor was invited to present his case.

"You can't gut an orange and put an apple inside and still call it an orange, Mr. Justice," he argued.

The case began on December 13, 2004. Eight days later, the judge ruled in favour of issuing marriage licenses to same-sex couples in Newfoundland and Labrador.

"I like the pastor's analogy of the apple and orange," said the judge. "But instead of putting one inside the other, I'm going to put them side-by-side under the umbrella of equality."

The courtroom erupted in cheers.

"Order, order in this court room!" the judge shouted.

We barely heard the sound of the gavel hitting the wood.

The couples embraced one another in tears, and their family members and friends shouted joyfully. Some people even danced. I was elated. Not only had we come a long way as a community, I had come a long way personally. I was always proud to be a Newfoundlander, but for the first time, I was proud to be gay.

Outside on the steps of the courthouse a scrum of reporters asked me for a comment.

"It all came down to the fruits, in the end," I said.

The next day, the lawyer emailed me a scanned copy of the order from the judge. I printed it and went straight to my mother's house.

"Look, Mom—now I *can* marry the person I love," I said.

She threw her arms around me and we cried together. Not because we were sad.

TOOLS

I was eight when my paternal grandmother said, "Me and your grandfather have knots in our stomachs worrying about you and your father." I heard that line every day until she died four years later. And it was only then, when she stopped speaking, that I finally listened and understood.

My people came from the old country. Like many families at the time, they left Ireland quite literally for bread and, when they arrived here, had to settle for crumbs. They weren't merchants. They worked with their hands. Their sharp humour cut through the hard times, and their stories and songs were passed down from one generation to the next like a coat of arms. It is in this ritual of *passing down* that we become equipped for things to come.

I didn't think it was fair that my grandmother kept me inside while the other children were outside playing. I remember hearing them on the street, their laughter echoed through the window like a loud drum that hurt my ears. I didn't want to learn how to cook, and I never liked doing dishes. The water made my hands look shrivelled and old. Getting down on my hands and knees to clean felt uncomfortable. Making the beds, doing laundry, and ironing clothes seemed like pointless tasks because they would have to be done again the next day.

One day, as my grandmother was walking me to the bus stop, I looked up at her and wondered why she was making me do this on foot in a half hour when my father could drive me to school in ten minutes. I burned with anger for her then, and now the fire of self-sufficiency, which she instilled in me, is what keeps me alive.

My grandmother died when all the chores were done. She finished her tea and lay down on my bed to rest, and didn't wake up. She had a heart attack. My grandfather followed her six months later. When they were gone and I was left alone with my father, I remembered what my grandmother said to me, but more importantly, I remembered what she taught me.

My father drank too much. And when he couldn't get out of his own bed, I knew how to get out of mine. I even knew how to make it. When he couldn't cook, I knew how to turn on the stove and prepare our food. And when he couldn't drive me to school, I knew how to get there myself, wearing a uniform that was washed and neatly pressed.

Sometimes, as feminists, we make assumptions about women like my grandmother because of how they chose to live their lives. In doing so, we create our own brand of fundamentalism. Instead of using gender as a bridge, it divides us even further. Where do we go from here? And how do we get there?

The answer isn't in the dismantling because we can't throw it all away, as much as we'd sometimes like to. It's in the rebuilding, not just of material things or abstract ideas, but of people and communities. How do we do this? We work together and salvage whatever supplies we can, using the tools we've acquired as our base. I think we can learn a lot from women like my paternal grandmother. Was she teaching me how to be a devoted housewife? No, of course not. She was teaching me how to survive in the only way she knew how. And those methods of survival are practical tools. She taught me how to be independent and how to care for myself in a way that would see me securely into the future. And I have used those tools to build my foundation.

COLONIAL STREET

Melancholia is most annoying. I learned how to lament early on, and I was ridiculously good at it. Longing latched on to my heart and refused to let go. Or maybe it was the other way around. Oh the yearning. Woe to me. Barf.

Now there have been periods in my life when I've experienced real depression, but that's not what I mean. And there may have been a woman or two or three who I went mad for, but that's not what I'm referring to either. I missed Ireland. Deeply. It was my homeland, after all. I wasn't born there, nor did I reside there for any length of time. Oh and I've also never been there. Except in songs. I inherited this affliction from my mother's brothers, who sang Irish ballads at every family get-together. When his father lost his voice to throat cancer, my Uncle Tony became the voice of Irish immigrants everywhere. The water was indeed wide. When he sang, he would close his eyes and, I swear to God, the man thought he was transporting us all in St. Brendan's leather-clad boat back to the old country. Seriously. He acted as though we never left.

The type of nostalgia I grew up with is common among those Newfoundlanders who feel a kinship with Ireland because that's where their ancestors came from. But sentimentality doesn't move us forward. In fact it keeps us stuck in the past and reaffirms the construction of binaries. It's why we think in terms of Catholics versus Protestants, and that sectarianism settled right here with us. We may have been colonized by the English, but what we Irish Catholics don't seem to account for is that we came over here too, and are therefore culpable in the seizure of Indigenous lands. It's impossible to feel nostalgia for that past.

The body of water that surrounds Newfoundland is not only lined with the scars of foreign trawlers, it's a cemetery full of unmarked graves. Our ancestors risked their lives to live here. The fishery and the seal hunt have claimed the lives of countless Newfoundlanders and Labradorians. Colonization claimed the lives of an entire Indigenous nation and culture—the Beothuk. The Mi'kmaq, the Inuit of Nunatsiavut and NunatuKavut, and the Innu of Nitassinan continue to struggle for fairness and equality.

Newfoundlanders and Labradorians often have a tendency to romanticize their history of hard times because so many of our traditions, our songs, and even our cuisine are rooted in our ability to survive. Islanders celebrate and identify strongly with our physical landscape and our history, but in doing so we risk becoming oblivious to our past mistakes and resistant to change.

I remember a colouring book I was given when I was in Brownies. It showed Sir Humphrey Gilbert triumphantly arriving in St. John's, taking possession of the island for Queen Victoria I in 1583. The package of crayons I was using actually contained a crayon called Flesh, which resembled the colour of my skin, Caucasian. I put up my hand.

"Miss, why is there only one colour for skin?" I asked.

"Just colour the Indians brown or black," she answered.

At the time, I was struggling with how to colour the two Indigenous people in the Newfoundland Coat of Arms, an image that was also included in the colouring book. The depiction of two Beothuk warriors, of course, is an interpretation of the British illustrator. A shield is placed between the two Beothuk, who are holding it in their hands. A white or silver cross, supposedly a reverse take on the Cross of St. George, divides the shield into four quarters consisting of two lions and two unicorns, linking Newfoundland to the United Kingdom. There's an elk or a caribou located above the shield and perched on a ribbon that also links Newfoundland to England. The motto located underneath the shield is *Quaerite prime Regnum Dei*, from Matthew 6:33: "Seek ye first the kingdom of God."

But really, there was only one kingdom—the British Empire. The Beothuk were native to Newfoundland and are now extinct. Shanawdithit was believed to be the last of her kind.

The company who manufactured the crayons later discontinued the Flesh colour. In my opinion, it should've never been developed to begin with. And as for the coat of arms, they were formally granted in 1637, adopted in 1928, but as of 2018, the provincial government has put plans in motion to have it redesigned with input from Indigenous people because the official description of the Beothuk in the arms refers to them as "savages."

There are two prominent memorials in the capital city's downtown public common, Bannerman Park. The first one was erected in 1889 in honour of a priest named Michael Morris, who apparently singlehandedly nursed orphans suffering with typhoid until he succumbed to the illness himself. The second one is the Shanawdithit memorial. Shanawdithit was captured in 1823 and, in 1828, was brought to St. John's where she lived as a servant until her death in 1829. She died of tuberculosis. Apparently she frequented the grounds, since she lived nearby, but I find it rather ominous that her memorial is placed mere steps away from the Colonial Building—the former home of the Newfoundland government and House of Assembly, which has recently been restored.

I actually live on Colonial Street, just within walking distance of that massive colonial symbol.

The Colonial Building hosted many galas, exhibitions, even protests and riots. It has a rich political history as well—the winning of Responsible Government in 1855 and the inaugural National Convention in 1946, for example. The cost of construction was expensive back then as the facade was fashioned out of white Irish limestone with six sizeable phallic columns. However, the cost to restore it was far greater. In addition to refurbishing the inside of the building, construction crews worked non-stop, cutting down old trees and tearing up the landscape around the area to ensure the building and its grounds would more closely resemble the past.

I'm proud to be a Newfoundlander and the descendant of Irish settlers who sought a better life and the freedom to express their faith on another continent. But I'm not prepared to accept my cultural past without recognizing the disastrous mistakes of that past. I've heard arguments to the contrary, qualifications and excuses, but I see what happened to the Beothuk as nothing less than genocide. And I am unwilling to accept an identity which remains blind to historical cruelty, an identity hoodwinked by nostalgia.

When we accept an individual identity, we inevitably become a part of a larger group. But larger groups tend to set the boundaries of our identities; they decide what behaviours and attitudes are acceptable. And this attempt to control people can lead to uniformity and stagnation. When an individual challenges the group with whom they identify, they can inspire change or run the risk of being cast aside. I was beginning to think that many of the beliefs passed down to me were far more imagined than real. And even though my identity didn't seem clear to me at the time, even though something didn't feel exactly right to me and that I was only learning it as I went along, I was at least ready to start challenging the dominant group. What I discovered is that some people are willing to expand their identities to embrace others. And some people will cast you out.

HOPE WALK:
GRAND FALLS TO GANDER

DAY 19

The steady pound of my feet on pavement was rhythmic, as though I were walking into battle, but it felt like I was actually walking out of one. And with each step forward I knew I was getting closer—not just to the finish line, but to some greater understanding of myself.

The highway was still. A wave of golden sunlight bathed the entire landscape, so I paused for a moment. The caw of a lone crow prompted me to bellow my name at the top of my lungs as if to let it go. When the echo returned my name to me, I knew I would never let it go.

My heart was in St. John's. It was Pride Week, and for the first time in years, I wasn't able to attend.

Facebook Post: "Day 19 and it's also the start of Pride in St. John's! This is the first year that I won't be speaking at City Hall because of

my cross-island walk, but I'm proud as ever.
March on dear friends! I am with you. Always.
Happy Pride!!!"

As I was walking, a man in a white pickup truck pulled over to say hello. His voice had a rugged drawl, but his smile was warm and engaging.

I've been in the media steadily for well over a decade as an advocate for LGBTQ2+ rights and more recently as an advocate for survivors of clergy abuse. And advertisements ran frequently about my walk over the airwaves in addition to all of the media interviews. Wherever I went in the province, people recognized me.

"Not gunna make it to town for Gay Pride?" he asked.

"This year I'm celebrating Bay Pride," I told him.

He laughed and handed me a twenty-dollar bill through the window as a donation.

"I'd march with you any day," he said. "Me young fella is gay and you saved his life."

With the exception of that first man in Port aux Basques, it seemed as though big, burly men were my biggest cheer-leaders on the road. Many of them brought me coffee, which I'd sip while sitting in the cab of their pickup trucks listening to their stories about how they struggled in their personal lives based on the abuse they endured. Some of them even wanted to introduce me to their daughters, which, I must admit, was very flattering.

One man told me he was wary of taking the anti-depressants his doctor prescribed, so I opened up to him about my experience with anti-depressants. I told him that, a few years ago when a bishop's assistant contacted me, I was re-traumatized to the point that I experienced anxiety and depression. When my doctor prescribed anti-depressants, I had to remind myself that it isn't any different than taking medication for the flu.

"There's no shame in spending some time with Auntie Dee," I said.

His laughter filled him entirely, to the point that it had to be released as tears. Moved by his vulnerability, I became teary-eyed, too.

He retrieved a handkerchief from his back pocket and proudly presented it to me.

"My wife just washed this," he whispered in a voice as soft as the fabric against my cheek.

I found his gesture comforting and recalled that my grandfathers, who also carried handkerchiefs, often wiped my face with them.

I asked him if I could keep it to remember him by.

"Thought I'd sell that on eBay after you used it," he joked. "But it's yours if ya wants it."

Midday I stopped to do an interview on VOCM. I talked about the challenges I faced and my progress so far. I also promoted the event at the end of the walk. VOCM was a sponsor, and Peter Soucy, who interviewed me, would emcee.

Facebook Post: "Just had a grand chat with Peter Soucy on VOCM's Back Talk about the Hope Walk Finale on August 2nd at the Mount Cashel Memorial. Keep watching for details!"

Gaining on Grand Falls, I completed another two intervals. My resolve was unshakable now.

DAY 20

I had travelled over 420 kilometers by foot when we said goodbye to my mother and uncle in the parking lot of the Mount Peyton Hotel in Grand Falls-Windsor—the designated location to switch out team members. The trailer was at Notre Dame Provincial Park in Lewisporte. I still had more than halfway to go, and there were only twelve walking days left, which meant I'd have to walk more than forty kilometers each day, regardless of weather or any other physical complications.

When I hugged my mother, I didn't think she would ever let me go. Her eyes filled with tears as she blew me a kiss and reluctantly got into her truck to head back to St. John's with my uncle. I waved at them as they drove off just as Shane Monahan and Clayton Handrigan arrived. Shane was one of the trainers who helped me prepare for the walk. He was joining me for five days. Clayton was the new driver and remained with me until the end.

We called Clayton "Santa Claus" because his hair and beard were white and his belly shook when he laughed. His voice was hefty and deep, yet his presence was light and unassuming, except when he played guitar. He took his guitar on the road, and whenever he sang, he magically transformed into country singer Kenny Rogers. After a successful thirty-year stint in education as a teacher, guidance counsellor, and principal, he held various positions as a driver. Born in Grand Bank, he lives in St. John's with his second wife, June. Even after twenty years of marriage, Clayton spoke about June as if they were still newlyweds. At seventy-four, he had a lot to talk about. He was proud of his three children and the way he and his ex-wife, who he referred to as his friend, ended their marriage.

Clayton drove us to an event that the Central NL Status of Women Council planned for me in Grand Falls-Windsor at Memorial United Church. Following the event, I had an interview scheduled with Kayla Fraser of *The Advertiser*, a community newspaper.

> Facebook Post: *"Day 20 and I can't wait to attend an event in the lovely town of Grand Falls-Windsor hosted by the Status of Women Council of Central Newfoundland and Labrador! I'll be speaking with a reporter from The Advertiser before I hit the highway again. Another full day, but I'm on the other side now and will be home soon!"*

When we arrived, Stephanie Bartlett from the Status of Women greeted us at the door and directed us to the auditorium. The room was filled with people from all walks of life. They applauded as I entered the room. A group of young peopled even lined up to get their picture taken with me.

Stephanie welcomed everyone and introduced Barry Manuel, the deputy mayor, who brought greetings on behalf of the town. Then Stephanie introduced me and invited me to say a few words. I thanked everyone for their support and talked about how pain can be transformative.

After I chatted with everyone over refreshments, I went outside for the interview. Clayton dropped Shane and I off on the Trans-Canada Highway shortly thereafter.

I could barely see Shane's eyes through his sandy brown, unkempt bangs when we first met. A moustache disguised his boyish face. His build was lean, and his smile too generous for limits. Ruggedly good-looking, he had an easy-going manner that made him approachable. I warmed to him instantly when he introduced himself at the gym.

I had just finished a workout with another trainer, Xi Hong, who was helping me prepare for the walk.

"I heard about what you're doing and I believe in it," Shane said. "Can I be a part of it somehow?"

Xi's demanding job was interfering with our training schedule, so Shane offered to train me on weights for the remaining six months.

The son of a professional musician, Shane taught himself drums at age ten and had his first professional gig at the age of fifteen in a local cover band, but had to get a note from his parents to play in the bar. Shane was often sought out to play drums for well-known St. John's bands. He played with Shanneyganock when he finished high school, but left after two years because life on the road wasn't conducive to the healthy lifestyle he had grown accustomed to. He was overweight as a child, but discovered weight lifting as a teenager, which eventually led him to pursue a career in the fitness industry. He has been working as a certified trainer ever since.

The clouds cast a light grey shadow in the sky. The air was cool, but it made Shane's first day of walking a little easier. When the day ended, he had to use a roller to work out the kinks in his legs.

"This is a tough grind even for me, and I train people for a living" he said.

We clocked thirty kilometers that day. I was still behind, but next to him I felt like I was on top of the world.

DAY 21

Clayton and Justin switched campsites to Jonathan's Pond Park in Gander after they dropped Shane and I off for the first leg of the day. Since my mother and uncle left, Clayton was charged with the set up and breakdown of camp, and Justin, in addition to coordinating with the team in St. John's, cooked and did laundry.

Shane and I started walking each day at 9 a.m. and at 2 p.m. we'd break until 4 p.m. Clayton would pick us up and take us back to the trailer to eat, change clothes, and rest. We'd begin the next leg at 4:15 p.m. and end at 8:45 p.m. I cut out breaks on the road. We clocked 31.5 kilometers that day.

As we were walking, a friend and colleague of mine pulled over to say hello while travelling to Conne River.

> Facebook Post: "Look at who I saw on the TCH! The lovely Tammy Davis, Executive Director of United Way. United Way has partnered with Pathways on two projects! And, Tammy and her parents made a donation to Hope Walk."

When people handed me donations on the road I'd give them to Justin to store in the safe at the trailer until we reached a town with a bank. Then I'd deposit the funds into the Pathways account.

DAY 22

We ducked as we headed to the truck, but there was no avoiding the rain. It shot out of the sky like bullets as we left the campsite and headed to my interview with CBC Radio in Gander. Following the interview, Clayton drove us to Cobb's

Pond. The Gander Women's Centre and Roads to End Violence were co-hosting an event for me.

Our team from St. John's made sure we had a steady supply of T-shirts to sell and often sent us a box from town.

Sometime during the planning stages of the walk, I received a telephone call from a dear friend who also happened to be my favourite Newfoundland artist, Gerry Squires. I thought of Gerry often as I walked, especially in the town of Gander, so close to his birthplace on Change Islands. But I also thought of him because his work so perfectly captures the rugged landscape of the island and the sense of deep time embodied in that landscape. He moved with his family as a boy to Toronto, where he attended art school, but eventually returned to Newfoundland to live in an abandoned lighthouse with his wife and two daughters in Ferryland.

Aside from his long list of awards, Gerry also received worldwide recognition. His work has travelled across Canada and beyond to such places as the United States, France, India, and Great Britain. He had a gentle old-world manner. His blue eyes swirled like his brush over canvas. Before he became terribly ill, he—alongside other prominent Newfoundlanders and Labradorians—made an appearance in the music video for the song "Pathways" by Pamela Morgan.

Gerry told me he was too ill to be by my side on the highway, but he wanted to make sure I had a piece of him to take with me on my journey. He generously donated an image of a hiker next to the ocean, climbing up a hill with no clear path forward. He told me I was the hiker and that it wouldn't be clear to me what type of journey I was on until I was in the thick of it. As usual, he was right.

Pathways custom ordered T-shirts from Living Planet, a St. John's-based business that specializes in silk-screening T-shirts and other informal attire. Popular throughout the city for showcasing a wide variety of designs by local artists, they now had an image by the legendary Gerald Squires to add to their gallery. His image became my shield. I would've gone to battle for Gerry. I wish I could've shielded him from cancer. We kept in touch throughout the walk. He'd send me supportive messages. He never let on how sick he actually was because he didn't want to distract me from the cause, which he firmly believed in. He died soon after the walk was over. Immortalized through his work. There wasn't a meadow, or a pond, or a cliff, or a little house on a hill, that didn't remind me of his art.

At Cobb's Pond, Sandra McKellar, the executive director of the Gander Women's Centre, welcomed everyone and introduced Sarah McBreairty, town counsellor, who brought greetings on behalf of the town. Sandra thanked Sarah and invited Lori Oram, the executive director of Roads to End Violence, to say a few words. Sandra thanked Lori and introduced me. I spoke about how the highway is symbolic of life. We often don't know where it will lead, but as we move forward we look to our past for guidance.

The room was crowded because of its size, but the windows made it feel expansive. I chatted with everyone over refreshments as they took pictures. I felt embraced by each town that hosted an event. The people I encountered reaffirmed how deeply the clergy abuse crisis affected this province.

Facebook Post: "Day 22 your rain poured out of the sky like a hailstorm. Thank you. It made me walk faster. A wonderful interview with CBC Gander and an event hosted by the Women's Centre and the Coalition Against Violence is how you began and I've been smiling ever since!"

Shane and I clocked thirty-four kilometers despite the rain and late start due to the event. I wasn't where I needed to be, but I still had time to change that.

THE GOOD PRIEST

You're not going to believe this. But it happened.

"I have to tell the bishop," said the good priest. As he leaned in closer, I could see pools of tears forming in his deep blue eyes.

As I sat in his office, across from him, I remembered years before when I went to the florist shop just down the road from his parish and ordered a single red rose to be delivered to him at the rectory. I loved fresh flowers. It wasn't unusual for me to show up and surprise loved ones with them. My response to the hardships in my life has always manifested through acts of impulsive and joyous rebellion.

I was thrilled when he referenced the rose in his homily at Mass that evening. He told parishioners that he placed it on the dining-room table in the rectory so that everyone who passed by could see its beauty. He said the rose was a sign from God because he received it on the Feast Day of Saint Therese, The Little Flower. She was the saint I prayed to after that. Her feast day, I discovered, was on my birthday. Every single time I said Novena to her, I saw a red rose on the final day.

The first time I laid eyes on him, I was hooked. His dark wavy hair dreamily shaped his polished face, and his angelic voice resounded throughout the church. When it came time for his homily, instead of hiding behind a podium, he delivered it in front of the altar. His youthful manner was as warm as his smile.

I want to be just like him, I thought to myself.

I wanted to be a priest when I was little. And even though I knew I couldn't be one, because I was a girl, I still felt called to God. I remember waking up in the middle of the night and singing out to my maternal grandmother who was fast asleep in the next room, "Nan, I feel like the Holy Spirit has grabbed hold to me and I'm going to do something special!"

"You're a special child, Gemma, but if you don't go back to sleep, you're grandmother's going to grab hold of you. Mind you, there'll be no room left for the Holy Spirit then."

Whenever she made homemade bread, she'd roll a handful of dough together to make a tiny bun just for me. Baking was like a religious ritual in her house. Her bread was so good; it may as well have been manna from heaven. She'd take out her tiny sherry glass, from her special cupboard on a separate wall in the kitchen, and pour me a little cup of apple juice. I'd use the bun and the juice to play Mass at her kitchen table. She'd say the words with me, correcting me if I misspoke. The transubstantiation had less to do with God and more to do with the love between us. It changed me.

The good priest wasn't long out of the seminary. It was too soon for him to be burdened by the sins of his church. That would come later. Charming and handsome, hordes of people gathered around him at the back of the church after Mass, but whenever I'd approach, he'd part the crowd and make way for me. I'd leap into his arms, and he would spin me around as if we were ballroom dancing. Was I a princess and he my knight in shining armor? I never wanted to be a princess, but I did want to be rescued.

I was in a lot of pain back then.

Before the good priest moved to another parish, he contacted a social worker. The principal at my school called me into his office, and the social worker was waiting for me there. I felt like her piercing eyes could see right through me. My body clenched like a fist when she asked me questions about my living situation. *Who will take care of my father once I'm gone?* I feared.

When school was over that day, I immediately went to the church and confronted the priest. He tried to explain to me that he was obligated by law to report what I told him, but I felt like he was just trying to cross me off his list before he left. But I couldn't have been more wrong.

Even though I no longer saw him, I thought of him often, especially after my suicide attempt landed me on the psychiatric ward at the Health Sciences Centre. I had just undergone months of intense therapy to try to change my sexuality. I had a second chance at life, and I was going to take it. I decided to write to him and tell him I was gay.

His sister hand delivered his response. I remember reading his letter as I sat at the tiny desk in my hospital room. There was no judgment, only love in his words. He ended his letter with, "Don't let your fear paralyze you." It moved me.

No one knew this at the time, and even I had forgotten about it, but before my suicide attempt, I had written another letter, at Christmas time, to someone else:

Dear God,

I'm so sad. I'm struggling with a lot right now. And there's too much pain in this world. I wish I could do something to change things. I go to Mass once a day and pray each morning and at bedtime, but I don't have any answers. I read my Bible daily, but I'm not really sure that it reflects the reality of people living in this world today (no offense). I feel called to you, yet I don't know where to find you. Sometimes, I go to the chapel next to the Palliative Care Unit in St. Clare's Hospital. I found it when I was walking my Pop up and down the hallway before he died of cancer. The lights are never on and it's really quiet there. One time I was crying so hard that I got down on my knees in front of the statue of Mary the Virgin Mother and begged her to take my pain away. But she looked like she was in her own kind of pain so I don't blame her for not answering.

Ever since I was little, I knew you had a plan for me. I could feel it in my heart. I'm meant to do something great, but I don't know what it is exactly. I talked to my friend Father [---] and he said you'd reveal it to me when the time was right. I'm really grateful for him. I wish I could pay him back for everything he's done for me. I had to move in with my Dad and he hasn't been the same since his parents died. Come to think of it, I haven't either. They took good care of us. His drinking is worse than it's ever been. He destroyed the house, and his sisters had to come clean it up so I could live there. Father [---] called the social worker, but that just made me mad. I can't leave my Dad and go back with my Mom because I'm worried my Dad will die. I'm trying to make the best of it seeing as how it's your birthday. I put up the tree in the dining room and the lights in the front window just like Nan showed me, but he just sleeps a lot. The lights are pretty and I thought it would cheer him up, but he hasn't left his bedroom.

And there's one other thing. I have a big crush on my friend Erin and I don't know how to get rid of it. I don't want you to hate me so I could really use your help right now. I wish you could send me a sign.

Love, Gemma

I rolled that letter up so it would fit into an empty Coca Cola bottle, tightened the cap, and threw it off a bridge. I waited until the current from the river swept it away. I walked back to my house on the old railway bed and never looked back.

Twelve years later, on the good priest's birthday, I told him I'd visit him on the weekend to drop off his gift. He was now a parish priest on the southern shore, less than an afternoon's drive away.

"I actually have a gift for you," he said in a mysterious tone.

"But it's *your* birthday," I replied. "What is it?"

"You'll see when you get here."

I was intrigued, and by the time Friday came I couldn't wait to hit the road. When I arrived, he greeted me at the door and handed me an envelope. I started to open it up quickly.

"Be careful with it," he said as he took the empty envelope from me. "I want you to know how much you have given to me and to those of us who know you."

Confused by his comments, I proceeded to unravel the discoloured piece of paper gently, with both hands, and was shocked and embarrassed to discover it was the letter I'd written to God.

The good priest told me that a fisherman found the bottle on the beach. Most of the words were faded, but the priest's name was still clearly legible, so the fisherman brought it to him right away.

That bottle floated out to sea and travelled for twelve years until it reached him. By that time, he and I had become close friends. I was over Erin, and the other girl crushes that followed, and came out to my friends and family. Dad was sober, and Mom remarried. I was back in university after I finally admitted to my parents, with the help of the good priest, that a priest sexually abused me.

Reading that letter was like getting a message from my former self. And similarly, like that bottle, I'd travelled a great distance emotionally to arrive at a place where I was beginning to have a better sense of myself. By receiving that letter and returning it to me as a gift, the good priest reminded me how far I'd come. I didn't need a sign in order to find the right path because I was on it all along.

CLIENT H

An audience of plants embraced as I entered her office. They were scattered about and cheered me on without saying a word. A black-and-white striped Mexican rug lay on top of grey commercial carpet and below the wicker furniture, which was placed angularly. One chair and a loveseat were stuffed with bulky floral-printed pillows, a basket of smooth rocks crowned the glass coffee table next to a box of tissues and another small basket containing tiny cards. Her desk consisted of an old door on top of two wood horses. I was reminded of how my paternal grandfather taught me to saw wood on one that looked similar, many years before. Receipt books and papers neatly lined both sides of her desk, framing a laptop in the centre. On the wall directly above the desk was a cluster of post-it notes, below them were two pictures of children in dark wooden frames. A bright red filing cabinet stood at attention underneath. At the other side of the room, atop the mantle of an old coal fireplace, was a brass candleholder with three white candles unburned at the wick. Beside the fireplace was a shelf filled with books on Buddhism. The only author I recognized was Pema Chodron. There was a large clock on the wall.

The conversion therapist's office certainly wasn't as inviting; it was much more conservative. But there was a bohemian vibe to this one. This therapist wanted you to know her. To get a feel for what she was like. She treated her office like a home—a space to relax. Light grey-papered walls were enclosed by a door and trim that was painted a warm grey. Her office was located in a heritage home conveniently located right next to where my maternal grandmother lived. I immediately felt at ease.

"Hi, Gemma," she said with a smile as she turned to greet me in her big cushy desk chair. She introduced herself and invited me to sit wherever I wanted.

I chose to sit on the corner of the couch next to the bay window. It made me feel like I wasn't trapped, and even when she relocated her office years later, I still sat in that spot.

"Before we begin, I want to get this out of the way," she cautioned. "Don't hold it against me, but I'm a CFA."

She didn't sound like a typical Come-From-Away main-lander, so I wasn't surprised when I found out she was an American. Later on, I discovered she was raised Episcopal in an upper-middle-class Colorado neighbourhood. Her father was a drilling contractor and her mother a poster child for domesticity in the 1950s—beautiful, conventionally feminine, and faithful in her housewifery—hostess to lavish dinner parties for her husband's mid-western colleagues and devout mother to their four children. My new therapist had earned a Religious Studies degree at Middlebury College in Vermont and a master's in Social Work in St. John's. She moved to Newfoundland in 1977 with her then husband, who took a position with the provincial government.

"And even after my divorce, I didn't want to leave," she said. "My kids were settled and I just love the people here."

Her hair was fixed at the shoulders and almost as white as the cotton blouse which hung loosely around her thin frame. She wore Birkenstocks and blue faded jeans. She curled her legs up in the chair and wrapped a grey wool throw around her shoulders.

"Your friend the priest suggested we meet," she said. "He thought we'd hit it off."

"Yes, and I had no idea you'd be this good-looking," I flirted, suddenly certain she was a lesbian.

"Do you always flirt when you're uncomfortable," she challenged.

She caught me off guard and wasted no time seizing the moment.

"Let's get started," she insisted.

"I'm definitely a flirt," I said with a smirk. But I knew she could see through my armor.

"Well, in here you're safe," she said. "You can be whoever you need to be."

My palms started to sweat. I thought she could hear my heart because of how loud it was beating. My body was reacting as though she was an intruder who broke into my home. It felt like an alarm was blaring inside of me...BLEEP, BLEEP, BLEEP...my mind kept telling my body to vacate the premises, but something inside prevented me from leaving. I never felt safe anywhere. Not around my neighbourhood, in my home, or at church. I've always had to be on guard, and obviously I wasn't very good at it considering what happened to me. I collected myself and quickly changed the subject.

"Are you a lesbian?" I blurted.

"No, but I'm flattered you think so," she answered with a generous smile.

"I was sexually abused by a priest. Is there hope for people like me?"

"I see a lot of clients from Mount Cashel and victims of Father Jim Hickey," she replied. "That's why your friend the priest thought we should talk."

As a part of my settlement with The Archdiocese of St. John's, they agreed to cover the costs of my therapy for as long as I needed. After numerous sessions, my therapist received a request from the archdiocese for a report on my progress. My therapist attached the following letter to an email:

> *Dear Msgr. _____*
>
> *Enclosed please find a summary report on treatment with Client H.*
>
> *Client H was initially referred to me as a result of being sexually abused by a priest of the Archdiocese of St. John's.*
>
> *As is common with many survivors, she had difficulties with maintaining personal boundaries, taking appropriate responsibility for things that*

were within her control, feeling guilt for things that were not within her control (including the abuse), grief over the change in relationship with a priest she had considered to be a trusted friend, distancing herself and shutting down, and appropriate self-care. All of these issues have had a negative effect on her relationships with family and romantic relationships. In addition, because the abuse was at the hands of a priest, a person whom she trusted and felt connected with, she also had issues concerning her faith, and relationships with people in positions of trust.

The goals of therapy for Client H were, and continue to be, to assist her in determining and maintaining appropriate personal boundaries; to learn where her responsibilities lie, and where she is taking either no responsibility or inappropriate responsibility; to cease blaming herself for the abuse; allowing herself to feel her emotions instead of avoiding them; grieving her friendship with the priest, and developing appropriate trust in people.

Since that time, she has had periods when she has not attended therapy, periods when therapy was focused on current difficulties, and when she avoided dealing with anything relevant to the abuse, and periods when her life presented her with issues that were directly related to the issues emanating from the sexual abuse.

She has been able to work through much of the effect of the abuse on her relationship with her parents, and has done considerable work on learning to recognize and maintain boundaries, but continues to have difficulties establishing and maintaining them. She also continues to have difficulty assigning appropriate responsibility in relationships. It has only been recently that she has been able to feel any anger towards her perpetrator or to begin to really understand the full impact of how the abuse has affected her. Trust continues to be a major issue for her, both with friends and with significant others.

She recently ran into her perpetrator, and this has triggered some emotional upset for her and revisiting of the abuse, the relationship with him, and guilt issues.

She continues to work through these issues as they appear in her life, and to use her understanding of the effects of the abuse to help her negotiate her way through relationships. A major challenge for Client H is to learn how not to shut down in the face of strong emotions, and this, along with learning how to trust people, has been the topic of her most recent therapy.

It is always difficult to predict how long therapy with an abuse survivor will take as one's current life situation sometimes triggers abuse issues, and sometimes serves as an opportunity to work through old issues. Client H is attempting to understand her life in this context, and to put some of these issues to rest so that she can be in healthy relationships with *others and with herself. She has considerable self-awareness at this point, and feels she is continuing to benefit from therapy.*

When I moved to B.C., Client H requested that we continue to have regular sessions by phone. I have agreed to do so, in part because trust is a major issue for her and over the years she has come to trust me, and to trust that I have a good understanding of what underlies her concerns.

Not long after, my therapist received the following email from the executive assistant to the archbishop entitled, "Seeking to get in touch with Client H."

We would like to send a letter to "Client H," but of course, we do not know her name, address or any other details. Would you be kind enough to send me the name and address of "Client H?" Thanks for your help.

When my therapist responded, indicating that she was not permitted to give out the personal information of her clients, she was issued an official request for a detailed report on letterhead from the Office of the Vicar General. Attached to the letter were documents entitled "Progress Report."

Dear Ms._____

I understand from my review of the records held by the Archdiocese that you have been counseling "Client H" since 1996. At this point I request a report from you concerning the progress of "Client H," with a view to determining in what manner

*we should proceed in the care of this individual.
Please give us your assessment of the following:*

1. In light of:

*a. the issues that were presented at the time of the
original assessment,*

*b. the goals originally set for the therapy provided,
and*

c. the treatment plan drawn up at that time

*Please describe the progress and needs of "Client H"
as they have developed over time, and as they
present themselves at the present moment.*

*2. What are your recommendations on how to
proceed with "Client H" from this point forward?*

*3. What recommendations or insights can you give
us concerning a foreseeable date of termination of
treatment?*

*For your convenience we have included forms which
might be helpful in responding to our request.*

In response to this letter, my therapist attached an informal
letter to an email to the vicar general.

Dear Msgr._____

*Attached is a brief report related to therapeutic
services to Client H in the last year, as requested in
your letter. You are already in receipt of a more
detailed report from a similar request.*

*Throughout this year, I have worked with client H
on a weekly, and sometimes more frequent basis to*

deal with her current therapeutic requirements.

The current therapeutic needs of Client H have been severely influenced by the contact she received from a representative of the Archdiocese. This contact has left my client feeling a great deal of alienation, anger, betrayal and confusion. She has experienced periods of sleeplessness and anxiety and is currently on antidepressants. The contact initiated by a representative of the Archdiocese has triggered much of the feelings she thought had been resolved with regard to the abuse, and she has been working through these with considerable effort and difficulty.

I would expect that this work will continue throughout this year in the same vein as she attempts to work through and process these distressing feelings.

On December 19, 2013, I invited the archbishop, his assistant, and the good priest to a meeting. I broke down as I began to talk, but once I finished crying, I was able to explain to the bishop how their request for information invaded my privacy, disrupted my recovery, and dismissed the permanence of the damage done. Both he and his assistant apologized. I told them that instead of being held hostage by my anger, I used it as inspiration to help others and founded Pathways, a non-profit for survivors of religious institutional abuse. I encouraged them to be forward thinking, to look at the bigger picture, because we were all raised within the same institution and therefore connected in that we are all part of the same narratives—the one we were taught to believe, and the one that we are living in. We can't undo all the wrong that has been done, nor can we forget everything that's happened, but we can change our response. Once I discovered that I had the power to control my own narrative, I felt empowered to rewrite the script.

Twenty-two years have passed since that first therapy session. Many more sessions have followed as a result. Without therapy, I wouldn't be able to do the heavy emotional lifting my advocacy work requires. After my failed suicide attempt, I made a decision to commit to my life. I renew this promise to myself every single day. It's easy to give up. But when you're pushed to your emotional limit, you have the capacity to push back.

JESUS, MARY, AND JOEY

Two pictures hung side-by-side in the hallway on the top floor of my paternal grandparent's house. The main one was a three-dimensional image of Joseph R. Smallwood, the first premier of Newfoundland and Labrador. An older, more distinguished "Joey," as he is commonly referred to by Newfoundlanders, sat sedentary in a dark wooden chair wearing a black suit and tie and his signature black-rimmed glasses. With a haughty grin, his right hand hushed the lip of a world globe while his left hand relaxed against his cheek. Behind him was a large screen with an outline of Newfoundland and a blue curtain draped off to the side as if he were on stage. From what I recall, the picture was mass-produced for an election campaign that took place during the 1960s. Next to the picture of Joey was Jesus, a close second, looking ever so humble. His skin was as fair as his hair was blonde. A red sash adorned his white robe as he kneeled against a sizable rock formation that was flat on top like an altar. His hands connected his outstretched arms, and his head, encircled by a bright yellow halo, was lifted towards the sky as tiny beads of light fell like raindrops directly above him. At the age of six, I asked my grandmother how his robe could be so white if he was praying on the ground. She told me it was immaculate, and though I didn't understand what that meant, I accepted her explanation as if it were gospel. Just below the pictures were two books thoughtfully placed atop a small rectangular dark wooden table: *I Chose Canada*, by Joey Smallwood, and *The Bible*, by God. But the way my grandmother viewed Joey, he may as well have authored both.

– – – – –

The skin on my grandmother's forearm looked like melted plastic. She told me it was scorched when she rescued her baby sister from a house fire. She always wore slacks and short-sleeve blouses at home and her thick greyish-dark hair was usually tied up in a floral bandana. She rarely went out, but took pride in her appearance whenever she did. She didn't own many dresses, but the ones that hung in her closet fit neatly around her slender figure. I'd watch her as she'd sit in front of the mirror attached to her antique dresser and wrap her hair up in pink plastic curlers. She'd always apply a generous amount of hairspray from an aerosol tin before putting on her make up.

She was very private. I never knew much about her life growing up, except that her family didn't have much money. Her father, Richard Power, was a veteran of the First World War and made a living as a fisherman until he passed away at the age of fifty-six. Her mother, Elizabeth, died at the ripe old age of eighty-nine. She stayed at home to raise their seven children. My grandmother was the middle child. They lived in the small rural town of Mount Carmel in St. Mary's Bay, located on the south coast of the Avalon Peninsula. Beautiful wild rose bushes surrounded the little white three-room house nestled on a hillside. I often visited my great-grandmother with my grandparents when I was little and sat beside her on the daybed, which was next to the stove. Her hair was short, but thick with white curls. She often wore cardigans and long skirts. Her blouse was always buttoned right up to her collar. I playfully called her Nan Nan because she was twice my Nan. She'd tell me stories about my great-aunt Annie, who unlike her siblings remained in the town. Not only did Annie teach at the local school, she was also the postmistress and a well-respected member of the community, just like her husband, Jimmy, who was a firefighter.

When my grandmother first left St. Mary's Bay and moved to St. John's, she got a job as a live-in housekeeper. She met my grandfather while working there because his brother lived on the same street. After a short courtship, my grandfather proposed and, once they wed, they rented a house in the west end of town. They bought their first and only house when my grandfather received a promotion at the Canadian National Railway. The house was located between two railway warehouses, which were connected by the railway track located directly behind their backyard. They never moved far from the railway station because, at that time, they didn't own a car. But as a railway employee, my grandfather received free passes to ride the train whenever they wanted to go anywhere outside the city.

Trains were a big part of my youth. I felt special because, whenever my grandfather would take me for a ride in one, I was allowed to sit up front with the conductor. I knew every conductor by name, and they'd always honk their horn whenever they'd pass by the house. I never got tired of counting train cars. Sometimes my grandfather would take me to his office and let me answer his phone: "Terra Transport, Hickey speaking. May I help you?" Terra Transport was an arm of the company operating exclusively in Newfoundland. My grandfather gave me a baseball cap with the CN logo on it, and my grandmother would have to pry the cap off my head in order to comb my hair before bed. I missed the trains when they were gone. It made everything else seem louder. When the Trans-Canada Highway was completed in 1965, it caused a decline in railway usage, and in 1988 it was discontinued.

Like most women from her generation, my grandmother managed the household and cared for her three children while my grandfather worked. She'd never hesitate to make room for relatives and neighbours in need by laying down sheets on the sofa and turning the armchairs into makeshift beds. The house was always filled with the scent of baked goods. An excellent seamstress, she could often be found in the dining room at her Singer sewing machine. She also crocheted and refinished antique furniture. She would peer over her black-rimmed glasses on the tip of her nose, making her look like a stern schoolteacher, but when she danced, her mirth cascaded out of her and into the air like a steady invisible stream. She was a tidy step-dancer—a hint of her Irish pedigree. She taught me how to waltz to the legendary Newfoundland songster Harry Hibbs.

My grandparents had a cabin at Placentia Junction, about 100 kilometers outside St. John's, and just like their house, the cabin was only a stone's throw from the railway tracks. I spent most of my childhood summers there. The cabin was called Shady Rest. It consisted of two small rooms: a kitchen and a bedroom with bunk beds. There was no running water, and the outhouse was located in the woods behind the cabin. Kerosene lanterns lighted the cabin at night and wood chunks fed the belly of the old cook stove. Merle Haggard and George Jones frequently blared over the ghetto blaster while we played a game of Growl. My grandmother was a card shark, but every now and then, she'd let me beat her. I'd save the pennies I won and place them on the railway track in the morning, waiting in anticipation for the train to pass. When I'd rush to the tracks to collect my flattened pennies, I could still feel the trail of wind left behind by the train.

It was at the cabin that my grandmother gave me my first fishing pole. She preferred fly-fishing, but taught me how to cast my line using bait.

"Hold on to your pole like you're shaking someone's hand," she'd remind me. "Bring your rod forward with your wrist, not your elbow," she'd caution.

She boasted to anyone who would listen on the day I caught my first trout. And she kept it in the deep freeze for seven years. She'd go fishing for hours at a time. I'd watch her from the tracks as she stood at the foot of the pond below in her bright blue coat and waist-high army-green rubbers. I was anxious to throw rocks in the pond, but couldn't do it while she was fishing. Sometimes, my grandfather would join me on the tracks and remind her to be careful.

Her name was Agnes, but my grandfather called her Ag. The way he pronounced her name sounded like he was saying Egg. He also called her his buddy. The priest used that in his homily at her funeral. Theirs was a bond like no other—the kind that blooms out of romance and outgrows hardship.

"Now, Ag, there's a drop a few feet out so be careful," he'd warn her.

"I know, Hick," she'd reply. "I'll be in after a few more flicks." Which would mean another hour at least.

Dusk would fall before she did. I could hear the whip of her line cut through the air. There was no electricity, so when it got dark you couldn't see your hand in front of your face. She'd still be at pond side. I'd have to go fetch her with a flashlight. Then we'd all play the game spotlight.

During the daytime I'd check the rabbit snares with my grandfather, fetch water from the well, split wood, and tend the land. Then he'd take me swimming. My grandmother watched in a lawn chair from the tracks and would wave at me whenever I looked in her direction. Those were some of the happiest times of my life.

I remember being afraid of bears because I overheard my grandfather mention to my grandmother that one had been spotted close by. One night, when I couldn't hold my pee any longer, I woke my grandmother up to take me to the outhouse. She took me by the hand and gave me the flashlight to shine on the path.

"Nan, are you afraid to die?" I asked as she marched us through the woods without fear.

"No, sweetheart. I'll face my Maker when I'm called."

"Nan, do you think the bears will get us?"

"No, sweetheart. But if you don't hurry, the fairies might."

I had just recently heard the word *fairy* from a boy whose grandfather owned the cabin next to us. He told me that fairies were pretty men who were light on their feet. So when my grandmother mentioned fairies, I thought I was going to be swept away by beautiful male dancers. But she was actually referring to tiny creatures of folklore that were supposed to be scary. Beliefs that fairies caused strange occurrences were common all over the island, but I think it was a creative way to keep children from straying too far. My grandmother's mother told her to take a slice of bread whenever she went berry picking in the woods to ward off the fairies or, as they were sometimes called, the little people. It was bad luck not to believe in them. And apparently, if you ever walked on a piece of land that was claimed by the fairies, you'd get struck with one of their arrows. This was the explanation given for unexpected irritations to the skin, like a boil. If the boil became infected, don't be surprised if twigs or feathers came out when lanced. It was believed that supernatural forces caused illnesses where my grandmother came from. She used home remedies and was sceptical of modern medicine. I think that's what killed her in the end because she didn't follow the doctor's orders when it came to treating her diabetes.

"Put iodine on it," was her answer for pretty much every ailment. Occasionally, when I had a cut or if she nicked Amy the dog when trying to trim her fur, she'd generously apply either iodine or mercurochrome. At least I had clothes to cover it up, whereas poor little Amy, whose fur was as white as snow, would have to go out into the neighbourhood with dark orange spots on her body. She looked like a polka-dot piñata.

My grandmother was a luminous presence in my life, and Joey Smallwood loomed as large as an icon in hers. So I was always mindful of the pictures of Joey and Jesus as I passed through her hallway, quietly tiptoeing along so as not to attract attention. One year however, when my grandfather gave me a water pistol for Easter, Joey's image appeared particularly shiny. In my mind it resembled a bull's eye, so I decided to use it for target practice. I had it timed perfectly. If I ducked behind the stair rail at the exact moment his image was shifting, I wouldn't get caught. Or so I thought. As the steady stream of water poured down the picture and onto his holy book, my grandmother was leaving her bedroom. "Jesus, Mary and Joseph," she yelled. I thought that Joseph was Joey until I found out later that she was referring to the father of Jesus and not the Father of Confederation. There were no pictures of Mary in the house, though her name seemed to come up a lot accompanied by the phrase, "The Virgin Mother." I was told *virgin* meant that God put a baby inside her stomach, so it never occurred to me that Joseph was Jesus's father. When my grandmother took the water pistol away, I knew that not even Jesus himself could save me. She put me over her knee and, in the acceptable fashion of the time, spanked me on my backside. My grandfather, who promised to take me to the cabin on a hunting trip, consoled me.

Fall came, and I set out on our big adventure with my grandfather by train to the cabin. When we passed through small communities, children ran alongside the train and waved at me as I peered out the window. My grandfather told me that Joey walked across Newfoundland on the rail bed to reach out to families who lived in rural parts of the island. He added that when Joey brought Confederation to Newfoundland, my grandmother's family benefitted from the social programs that were introduced because they lived around the bay. I adored my grandfather, so I told him that I could walk across Newfoundland to help people, too. To which he responded, "Gem, anyone who challenges Joey Smallwood to a dual can walk across Newfoundland."

And thirty-two years later I was on the Trans-Canada—the highway that replaced the railway—walking across Newfoundland in an effort to reach out to people isolated by the church because of the abuse they suffered at the hands of clergy.

HOPE WALK:
GAMBO TO CLARENVILLE

DAY 24

As Shane and I approached Gambo, the image of the man who brought Confederation to Newfoundland, Joseph R. Smallwood, in his signature black-rimmed glasses and bow tie, was mounted on top of an altar of pressure-treated wood with the text, "Joey's Lookout," emblazoned underneath his image, which was strategically positioned to look in the direction of the town. Smallwood was born in Mint Brook, near Gambo.

Seeing the sign brought back memories of my paternal grandmother. I told Shane that she placed Joey's memoir, *I Chose Canada* next to *The Bible* in her house.

"Remember that 3D portrait of Smallwood?" he asked. "I think every household had one of those."

"I used it for target practice for my water gun when I was six," I responded. "Until my grandmother caught me red-handed and then reddened my arse."

Shane laughed and told me that when he was six he got in trouble at school for throwing his classmates new hat in the toilet. The boy told their teacher and Shane was brought to the principal's office. The principal told Shane he was going to call his parents, so when Shane went home that day, he unplugged the phones from the jacks. He got busted when he told his mother that she wouldn't be taking any calls that day.

Gambo wasn't entirely visible from the highway, but as we edged closer, the panoramic view of Freshwater Bay impelled us to breathe sharply. The picturesque town was encased in a white, sunless sky as if it were held in a snow globe. I pointed towards the old railway bed in the distance. From the hill, it resembled one that came in a toy railway set.

As we walked back towards the highway, Shane told me to pose under the Smallwood sign.

"You were born for politics," he said, while he looked at me through the screen of his phone.

He wasn't the first person to say that.

Shane didn't know me when I entered provincial politics in 2007. I ran for the New Democratic Party on two occasions: first in a February by-election and later in the October general election. Even though my family members were card-carrying Tories, I decided to run for the NDP, which meant I had to come out to my family three times: first as a lesbian, second when I converted to the United Church, and third when I became a New Democrat. Honestly, the last two caused more of a stir than the first.

My election bid was unsuccessful as I came third in Kilbride, but I knew it would be a difficult race to win. Even though I had a public profile, I was an out lesbian running in a rural area. And John Dinn, the Progressive Conservative candidate who won, was a town councilor in the district before the area was amalgamated with the city of St. John's. He was also from the district and lived there. Nonetheless, when you know you're going to lose, you've got everything to win. I had experience running municipal, provincial, and federal campaigns, but never as a candidate, so when the late Nancy Riche, a well-known labour-rights activist who was also provincial party president at the time, invited me to run in the by-election, I welcomed it as a learning experience in order to prime myself for the provincial election.

In a by-election, because there's usually one race, the party's resources go to the candidate, so it was a great opportunity for me to get my feet wet and soak up everything the party had to offer. When the time came for the general election, I was ready to roll. I ran in the district of St. John's East. I lived in the district most of my life, the majority of my family and friends lived there, and I went to Gonzaga, which was a prominent Catholic high school, before the non-denominational school system was introduced, located in the heart of the district. I knew I had a shot. But I ran during a time when Danny Williams' popularity was at an all-time high. This time I had a much better showing and came second. The Progressive Conservative candidate, Ed Buckingham, won. Ed was a friend of mine, so it was a fun race. He and I worked on Shannie Duff's municipal campaigns together.

Running in two elections that year took a toll on my already strained marriage. By the time the 2011 election came round, I was dealing with the aftermath of a divorce. I gave the green light to another candidate, George Murphy, to run in the area, and he ended up winning.

Peter Stoffer, NDP Member of Parliament for Sackville-Eastern Shore, a district in Nova Scotia, flew to St. John's to campaign with me in Kilbride. After he spent the day with me, he told me he wanted to change the name of the party to the NGP—The New Gemma-cratic Party. A month or so later, I read an article in *Wayves*, a popular Atlantic LGBTQ2+ newspaper based in Halifax, where Peter was interviewed. He told the reporter that while in Newfoundland, he became a New Gemmacrat.

Peter and I had a lot of fun campaigning together in front of Bidgood's, a popular locally owned grocery store in the district. He was an excellent constituency person and had a book full of the names and numbers of people in his district. He'd call them on their birthdays. I learned so much from him.

Going door-to-door with Alexa McDonough in St. John's East was another campaign highlight. When she was elected leader of the Nova Scotia New Democratic Party in 1980, she became the first woman in the country to lead a political party. And she would go on to lead the federal party in 1995. We visited houses in a new subdivision across from the former location of Mount Cashel. At each house, she'd knock on the door, and when someone answered she'd introduce herself by name only, but when she introduced me, she'd list my credentials and accomplishments as if she knew me since birth. I'd speak after the introductions, and when I finished, she'd hand the person my flyer. I felt her eyes on me as I spoke with constituents. Peter impressed me, but I was overawed by Alexa. I followed her career for years. So her feedback was that much more important to me, especially as a woman.

"Gemma, when you give someone your attention, you make them feel like they're the only one in the world, and that's a real gift," she told me as we walked down another driveway.

I learned a lot from spending time with Peter and Alexa, but Shannie Duff was my true mentor. Over the course of her thirty-six-year career as a politician—in addition to her previous roles as a nurse and mother of five—Shannie served the city of St. John's as mayor, deputy mayor, and councillor-at-large.

As I lobbied for same-sex marriage in Canada, I sent emails out to influential people in my hometown to garner support for the cause. Shannie was one of the first to respond. When we met she was already aware of my advocacy work and was keen to offer her support. We became fast friends. I worked on her municipal campaigns, and when she had back surgery, I rotated nights with her children to help her husband with dinner prep. One time, as I helped her out of bed to use the washroom, her pajama pants slipped down. I was horrified for her because I thought she'd be embarrassed. But as usual, she didn't miss a beat.

"Not a bad ass for an old broad, hey?" she said. "And you've likely seen a few."

When she recovered from her surgery she insisted I loan her my pedal bike so she could learn how to ride again. Her husband and I both expressed our concern that it was too soon, but it was difficult to say no to her. We stood in the parking lot at The Rooms (the provincial art gallery) and watched her as she took off. Her laughter propelled her forward and she glided through the parking lot and then onto the street. When she waved goodbye to us, her husband turned to me and said, "Think she'll ever come back?" She was truly unstoppable. And we've shared many challenges and triumphs over the years.

I lived for the adrenaline rush of being on the campaign trail and relished interacting with people while going door-to-door, but the behind-the-scenes pettiness of party politics repelled me in the same way as the heckling that occurs in the House of Assembly. Whatever happened to witticisms and skillful debate?

I've always been passionate about politics. Ever since I was little, my favourite pastime with my father was going to the children's library in the basement of the Arts and Culture Centre. After I picked out the books I wanted to take home, he'd buy me a hot dog and a Pepsi at the canteen. We were there so often that all of the staff knew me by name. They always gave me a refill for free.

I picked books on all of the American Presidents, especially John F. Kennedy—the first Catholic President—though his brother, Bobby, was my favourite Kennedy. When it was election night in the United States, my father and I would watch the results on television in the same way we'd watch a hockey or baseball game—talking and gesturing at the screen while sitting on the edge of our seats.

The advocacy work I do requires me to network with politicians from all political parties, and I see so much value in working together for a common good. Sometimes, there are matters that are more important than individual aspirations and egos.

Shane left after we finished the first interval of the day. The weather was erratic during the five days that he walked with me. One minute the sun peeked from behind a cluster of clouds, and the next minute the rain gushed from the sky like a waterfall. He waded through all of it with me. There was no shelter on the open highway, but we took refuge in one another. At times we talked non-stop about growing up in St. John's, our families, and our hopes for the future, but then there were other times when I had nothing to say because I had given my all to everyone else. He steadied the silence. And though he was four years younger than me, I looked to him like an older brother.

> Facebook Post: "Thanks for rockin' five days with me on the TCH, Shane! Best core workout ever...laughing so hard never hurt so good! Get some rest now."

After a short break, I met Sandy Collins—MHA for the district of Terra Nova and Minister of Child, Youth and Family Services—on the highway. Sandy walked five kilometers with me. While we waited for his assistant at E.S. Spencer Bridge on the Terra Nova River, he handed me a personal check for one hundred dollars.

"This isn't an easy endeavour you've taken on," he said. "Good luck and take good care of yourself while you're out here."

He waved at me as he drove off, and I was alone again, but as I got closer to the person I could feel myself becoming, I started to enjoy my own company more. I was already feeling like I made it home in a way—walking from one side of the island to the other side of myself.

DAY 25

As I came upon a river in Terra Nova Park, I noticed a small green space that was constructed into a picnic area. There was a large swing set pitched on top of a sand patch further back closer to the woods, and a picnic table next to the river. In order to get to it, I'd have to walk through a small parking lot and along a trail. Every step counted while I was on the highway, and I tried to avoid additional walking as much as possible. So I chose to sit on the guardrail instead.

I pulled a protein bar from my backpack. But before I could take a bite, I noticed what appeared to be a fox coming out of the woods in my direction. As it got closer, it started to resemble a stray dog. But when it came within ten feet, I realized it was a coyote. I didn't have a stick, but it wasn't travelling in a pack, so I remained seated. I thought it best not to run. But when it came within five feet, I stood up slowly and stared directly into the animal's eyes. It wavered from left to right and eventually ran off.

Maybe I'd been out on the highway for so long that the coyote thought I was another wild animal. The hair was creeping up on my legs like vines. I hadn't shaved them in weeks, and the hair under my arms was so thick and bushy, it looked like I had two trees in a headlock. Layers of dust from the road caked my lower body, while the clothes on my upper body were saturated in sweat. My odour was musty. I was starting to blend into my environment. I was almost feral.

And there was freedom in that sense of near wildness. All my life, I had been domesticated. I moved from one category to another, trying to claim a sense of identity, so I could be received. But perhaps I was meant to be something *other*. I was learning how to take myself back because I knew I was never supposed to be tamed.

DAY 26

It was sunny and nineteen degrees when we left our campsite to head to Clarenville for an event that Paul Power, the assistant principal of Clarenville Middle School, and Jill Monk, a town councilor, organized for me at the Bill Davis Chalet. Before I entered the chalet, I did an interview with Mike Toy from VOCM.

> *Facebook Post: "Day 26 is a busy one! I'm heading to Clarenville for an interview with VOCM and an event hosted by the Town, then lots of walking with the one, the only, TA Loeffler!"*

When I entered the chalet, the room was full of people from the town. TA Loeffler, my lead trainer who was scheduled to walk with me that day, surprised me by meeting me there. Paul welcomed everyone and gave opening remarks before inviting Mayor Frazer Russell to bring greetings on behalf of the town. After Mayor Russell spoke, Paul invited me to say a few words. I looked out at the people assembled there and explained how the walk had surpassed my expectations because of the response I received from individuals as well as communities across the island. I expressed how important it is to bring issues like this out in the open so we can heal, not just individually, but collectively as well because when someone is abused, their mental health is compromised, and that impacts every other aspect of their lives as well as the society they live in.

When I finished speaking, Paul invited Jill Monk, Paul Tilley, and Mayor Frazer Russell up to present me with a check from the town. Jonathan Parsons of *The Packet*, a local newspaper, who would interview me after the event, took a picture for the article. After the event, Jonathan met TA and I on the highway to take more pictures. TA walked twenty-eight kilometers with me that day. When she met me in Clarenville, I had walked nearly 660 kilometers. With six days remaining and almost 250 kilometers left to go, I'd have to trudge more than forty kilometers each day. I stepped up my pace because my feet finally toughened, ate on the road, and stretched out the length of my walking times to maximize my results. And it worked. I had nearly achieved my initial target.

TA and I passed a benchmark on the highway.

"The walk is a benchmark in your life, signifying your healing and growth," she told me.

In order to complete the massive goal I set for myself, a walk of over 900 kilometers, I knew I had to engage someone who could train me both physically and mentally. There was only one person who could mentor me in the way I needed, and that was TA Loeffler.

TA's adventures have led her all over the world. A celebrated academic and award-winning adventurer, her lectures and keynotes continue to inspire. I was delighted when she agreed to prepare me for my walk and lead my team of trainers—there were four other trainers in addition to her: Shane Monahan, Philip Alcock, Xi Hong, and Audrey Hynes. We began training the first week of September in 2014. Each week, she'd send me a plan.

If I stuck with my original plan to do the walk in August, I'd need to go forty kilometers most days in order to have a few rest days, or go thirty-one kilometers a day for twenty-nine days straight, or some combination thereof.

If I stretched it to a five-week walk (i.e., thirty-six days) then my daily average would drop to twenty-five kilometers a day with no rest days, or thirty a day with six rest days.

So I needed to decide which combination worked best, especially considering that there would be media interviews and events, not to mention breaks for washroom, water, food, and people greeting me along the way.

In the end, I decided to do the walk in thirty days, from July 2 to August 2, with two rest days, which I didn't end up using after I fell behind due to an allergic reaction and other physical issues that arose without warning. Depending on how much pain I was in, I walked four to five kilometers an hour with roughly seven or eight hours of walking per day. But there were some days when I did less, and that meant I had to make up the kilometers on another day. I took an entire year of annual leave from work to do the walk within this timeframe. I work as the Executive Director for an arts-based youth charity called Artforce (formerly named For the Love of Learning), where we boost the employability and self-esteem of at-risk youth through creative programming and projects.

Part of my training routine during the winter months involved pulling tires up Signal Hill. I remember one morning when I became overwhelmed with emotion. Tears began to form steady streams on both cheeks before I reached the top. Along with the tire, TA added weights to my backpack. It was cold, and the wind, unsympathetic to my cause, shook me from all directions. Though weighed down, I felt unearthed, exposed, not just to the elements, but also to myself. I thought about what was stolen from me when I was young—my innocence, my ability to trust others—and I also thought about the hurt I'd caused because I was sexually abused. And even though I broke down, I still kept going, my response to the adversity in my life.

When I finally reached the top, I told TA that I cried, but it felt very cathartic.

"You've been carrying this weight around with you for years, and you're letting go now," she said.

She reminded me that it was Shrove Tuesday, a day of repentance and reflection observed by Catholics. At that point, I hadn't been involved in the Catholic Church for years, but I couldn't help but chuckle to myself when I remembered the saying, "You can take the girl out of the Catholic Church, but you can't take the Catholic Church out of the girl."

Ironically, I could never really take the girl or the church.

RECIPE

"If she doesn't marry you, I will," I told her.

Her blonde hair loosened over her face like a broken wave in the wind.

"I think I may let you," she said.

Her cheeks flushed with colour. The gleam from her girlish grin flashed my eyes as she turned her head towards the sky. Things were looking up. Too bad we didn't pay attention to the Parks Canada sign that cautioned us not to go any further. Live and learn, I suppose.

And there we stood on the edge of an actual cliff at Cape Spear, ready to jump off a metaphorical cliff into the rest of our lives. We fell deeply, but it was too soon to know we would drown. Not even the lighthouse at the most easterly point in North America was able to warn us of the danger that lay ahead. Love is blind.

A week later, she left her partner to be with me. We were engaged within six months and married that same year.

That wasn't my first experience at the cape.

When I was eight, I pitched myself between the two front seats of my paternal grandfather's red Plymouth Horizon illegally parked next to the washroom in the lot at Cape Spear. I thought the name sounded cool, so I asked my grandmother if she knew where it came from. She told me the Portuguese named it Cabo da Esperanca, and the French called it Cap d'Espoir, which both mean Cape of Hope. But the English called it Cape Spear. I was curious to know why *hope* got lost in translation.

"Was it because the land shoots out like an arrow, Nan?" I asked.

"No, sweetheart."

"Was it because the rocks are like daggers?"

"No, darling. It's because the English were Protestants."

No hope for those poor old Protestants, I thought to myself. I sat back in the seat, keeping my eyes peeled on the door of the washroom and hoping my grandfather would come out soon. He promised to take us for custard cones on the way back into town at my favourite store, Lar's.

Named after its owner, Lar Crocker, the store wasn't designated a national historic site by the Canadian government like Cape Spear, but in the heart of us townies, it was a national treasure. And just like a signal from the lighthouse to a ship at sea, the flickering lights in the display window and a flash of that bright smile from Lar's wife, Winnie, made you feel like everything was going to be okay.

But Lar's closed years before she and I stood on that cliff

together. So did the lighthouse.

And I visited that site again on the day my divorce was finalized. As I stood on the cliff staring out at the vast expanse of the Atlantic, I removed my wedding band from my finger and tossed it into the ocean. *There's no such thing as a happy ending*, I thought. Otherwise why would it end at all?

My ex-wife was a Mennonite from Manitoba. Because Mennonites are pacifists, they fled the persecution they endured from Roman Catholics and Protestants, which resulted in them moving from place to place. Her family descended from Russian Mennonites because that's where they ended up before migrating to the western parts of Canada. Their ancestry was Germanic, and they spoke Plautdietsch, which means Mennonite Low German. In an attempt to impress my future mother-in-law, I incorporated some Low German into my wedding vows.

Unlike her parents and siblings, who accepted that she was in a same-sex relationship, her extended family, scattered throughout the prairies, were conservative Mennonites. During one of their family reunions at the Mennonite University in Winnipeg, her extended family members shunned us. When we'd enter a room, they would turn away. When we took a seat in the cafeteria, they would relocate to another table. This went on for a couple of days until one of them, a minister from Alberta, spoke up while we were gathered in a prayer circle.

"We have a crisis in this family," he stated. "And I for one can't continue unless we address it."

At that point, I had had enough. "Excuse me, but if you're going to reference me in such a manner, please acknowledge my existence by looking at me," I said.

He responded by quoting a particular translation of Leviticus 18:22: "You shall not lie with a male as with a woman; it is an abomination."

In my head, I was like, *Dude, really? If you hadn't noticed, I actually don't lie with a male like I do a woman.*

First of all, the Leviticus passage doesn't reference lesbians specifically, and in fact *The Bible* doesn't reference homosexuality either. The word appeared in English translations in 1946, according to Dr. David Bell, one of my former Religious Studies professors. Any biblical reference to homosexuality is up for debate because, as words get translated, meanings vary. Furthermore, when these references are placed within a wider cultural context, they actually have nothing to do with same-sex love.

Now, this minister from Alberta didn't know I had an undergraduate degree in Religious Studies or that I had reading knowledge of Latin and Hebrew. But he soon discovered that he was out of his league when it came to debating scripture.

I planned on pursuing a degree in Social Work when I started university because I was passionate about social justice and wanted to find a way to help people that could replace the call to ministry I had felt when I was younger. However, the first Religious Studies course I took with Dr. Jennifer Porter, as an elective, peaked my interest so much, it prompted me to change my major to Religious Studies instead of Psychology. Religion was always an interest of mine since stumbling on books by famous theologians in my father's study. And a background in Religious Studies provided me with an alternative to the limited faith perspective I was raised with. But more than that, it equipped me with knowledge to spar with those that opposed my very existence. I thoroughly enjoyed whenever Jehovah Witnesses came to my door. I'd invite them in, and as we sat and chatted in my living room, I'd casually let it slip.

On one occasion, for example, after making a pot of tea, I asked if they would like some more.

The two dapper young men, flawlessly dressed, replied in unison, "No thank you."

"Did I mention I'm a homosexual? Let me get you some more milk."

By the time I was back from the kitchen, they had made a beeline for the door, leaving one of their brochures on the coffee table.

The look on their faces was worth serving them tea in my paternal grandmother's fine china. Whenever religious fundamentalists flung Bible verses at me, I'd fling them right back like I did in Winnipeg at the reunion.

Leviticus provided structure and direction for a people that were literally on the move looking to put down roots and who also wanted to be different than neighbouring communities. There was no such thing as police back then, so religious laws were vital to ensure civility and survival. But in our society, religion isn't the law, and a deeper analysis of such passages reveals that they aren't about homosexuality as such. I wanted to enlighten this so-called minister and point out that the passage likely referenced incest or sex with a minor and that the hegemonic construal of his analysis is tricky because the original meaning of the text in Hebrew literally got lost in translation. But instead, I directed his attention to Leviticus 20:21:

> For no one who has a blemish shall draw near, one who is blind or lame, or one who has a mutilated face or a limb too long, or one who has a broken foot or a broken hand, or a hunchback, or a dwarf, or a man with a blemish in his eyes or an itching disease or scabs or crushed testicles. No descendant of Aaron the priest who has a blemish shall come near to offer the Lord's offerings by fire; since he has a blemish, he shall not come near to offer the food of his God. He may eat the food of his God, of the most holy as well as of the holy. But he shall not come near the curtain or approach the altar, because he has a blemish, that he may not profane my sanctuaries; for I am the Lord; I sanctify them.

Mennonite churches lacked the lustre of the Catholic churches I was accustomed to, but I honestly didn't miss the ritual. It seemed to me that Mennonites were secure enough in their faith that they didn't need to overcompensate by decorating their churches. The podium is the focal point, and there's no altar. Regardless, I asked this minister if the glasses he was wearing to correct the blemish in his eyes interfered with his ministry at all.

Even though my partner's parents ran a successful construction business, they never moved out of the city's notorious North End. Her mother was quiet, but solid to her core—a rock. She was the administrator of the family business. Her father worked construction alongside his employees during the week, except for Sundays when he was a lay preacher at their church. He was well read, and I quite enjoyed our heated discussions on theological discourse. Her parents relished their trips to Newfoundland. They were devoted fans of Buddy Wasisname and The Other Fellers and purchased many of the band's CDs. The first time we saw them on stage, I remember her old man and me sobbing to "Saltwater Joys." Mennonites and Newfoundlanders aren't that different, I concluded, especially after hearing some of their folk music and sampling their traditional food.

When I told my maternal grandmother that I was dating a Mennonite from Manitoba, she said, "What about that Quaker from Nova Scotia you were seeing before her?"

"She moved away to focus on her music career, Nan."

"You certainly knows how to take Christian love to a whole new level," she said, as her head cocked backwards with laughter. "Gives new meaning to the term missionary work, you do."

"Nan!" I shouted in disbelief.

I honestly thought my maternal grandmother would take me coming out as a lesbian better than me coming out as a Protestant. But, as usual, her response surprised me, "Same God over there."

Later, I was nervous about telling her that we were getting a divorce. But she surprised me with her response yet again.

"Gemma, there's the one you love, the one that loves you, and the one you marry."

Such wisdom in my grandmother's sayings—a life lived solely for others, her husband and nine children. I was a teenager when her cookbook, *My Personal Touch*, was published, so I wrote this to honour her:

Dearest Grandmother,

Recipe is defined as a set of instructions for making something, a formula or procedure for doing or attaining something.

Because of you and my grandfather, we're all familiar with the word recipe *in this family. And everyone at one point or another has heard the saying: "That's a recipe for success."*

When I think about love I think about you and all the things that you did each day for your family in order to make everything come together, like in one of your recipes.

Sometimes, you need more ingredients than love to make a marriage work. Selflessness, patience, and dedication are some of the ingredients you added to your marriage and just look at what you made!

This little poem is called "Recipe" and I wrote it for you...

She rests her apron upon the pantry door,
leaves the bread to rise
and waltzes a broom across the kitchen floor.

The clothes are washed and hung on the line.
Her husband's shirts pressed,
the hand-me-downs mended with twine.

The beds are stripped, the sheets aired.
The table is set,
and the food prepared.

Two children at her feet, and one at her breast.
Another in her belly,
her husband is blessed.

I always wondered what secrets she held dear. I'd never know because her heart was a precious jewel that would forever remain hidden in a chest full of treasures. At certain points in my life, I'd discover clues based on her adages, but they only lead me so far. I decided that the rest wasn't mine to know or even understand. And whatever my grandparents were to one another, I was so grateful to them for my mother. My cousins were like siblings to me. Growing up, I never felt alone because of them. I was an only child until my mid-teens when my mother remarried and her husband brought twin boys into the mix.

Food framed my family. My grandmother and her younger siblings were taken out of school during The Great Depression to help their single mother (their father had recently died) with cooking meals and selling them cheaply to relief workers. Each day, men would line the stairs towards their one bedroom apartment in downtown St. John's.

My grandfather's family, on the other hand, lived in a one-room shack on Signal Hill. Being dirt poor, he figured out at an early age how to dig deep. Each day he would walk down the hill and wait by the bakery. Impressed by the fact that he showed up at the same time each day, the owner of the bakery eventually offered him a job. My grandfather worked his way up the line and became their master baker.

I could measure my mother's upbringing and add the number of siblings, divide it by the times, and subtract the difference to measure the sum of my grandmother based on the recipes in the cookbook. The cookbook was a map of their life together.

What I understood by my grandmother's adage about marriage was that not all relationships are considered equal because it's not possible to love everyone in the same way. As I walked, I started to interrogate the institutionalization of love. Why is loved measured in the same way when every single one of us is different? It's because, from a very early age, that's what we're taught. And when it turns out to be different (i.e., when the script changes because our lives are living scripts) we think we've failed.

Speaking of scripts, I thought my former wife's family was perfect, and at times I was envious of her for growing up the way she did. But while her family may have seemed like the heteronormative Christian ideal, in reality they were the exception because the vast majority of families didn't look like that at all. There were married couples with children and without, common-law couples with children and without, single-parent families, same-sex families, and so on. You get my point. Because my family changed when I was little, I was noticing all different types of non-traditional families, including the Holy Family.

"Miss, do you think Joseph got mad at Mary for having Jesus with God," I asked my teacher during a religion class one day.

Shocked and appalled, she slapped my desk with a wooden ruler so hard the ruler snapped in half. She told me never to ask questions like that again because they were blasphemous.

So why did I want to desperately be a part of my former wife's family? Because it wasn't what I had growing up, and it was what I thought I was supposed to have. I was also naive to think that my ex-wife could save me, but Catholicism planted that script in my head, too. The notion that we need to be saved comes from religions rooted in heteropatriarchy, and it's also a mindset that continuously gets reinforced by coloniality and views of the nation state.

Newfoundland and Labrador is a clear indication. This province has never benefitted from saviours. Joey Smallwood is only one example. The idea that we can be saved by God, by anyone else but ourselves, strips us of our own agency. We become dependent on the idea, and our individuality gets lost in the collective script. The truth is we don't need anyone to save us. Besides, what exactly do we need to be saved from?

My ex-wife first caught my eye while speaking to community advocates at a reception following a December 6th Vigil. Her energy ignited me. Of course, when she smiled in my direction from across the room, I obviously took that to mean she liked me. I decided then and there that I would make her mine. I thought we would make an amazing team, that we could change the world together. But truly, over the course of our marriage, she and I were always a world apart. And that was on me.

I chose to propose to her on a day that honoured a clergyman who was apparently martyred by way of decapitation. Legend has it that St. Valentine performed weddings in secret for soldiers who were forbidden to marry during the reign of

Claudius II. The irony wasn't lost on me when our marriage finally ended. I suppose, like St. Valentine, we all die a little when it comes to love.

I took her to her favourite vegetarian restaurant and prearranged with the owner to reserve the little nook by the window—it was where we lunched the first day we spent together before going to Cape Spear. After we ate, I cued the owner to play our song, and as one of the wait staff presented her with the bouquet of flowers that I had dropped off earlier, I got down on one knee and asked her to marry me. I had the ring custom made, using the diamonds from my paternal grandmother's engagement ring. She said yes, and as we embraced, the restaurant erupted in applause. It was perfect until it wasn't.

For most of my life, I never thought I'd get married, even though I devoted years fighting for the right to do so. As a feminist, I believe a person has a right to choose, and though I remained conflicted about the patriarchal historicity of marriage, I felt strongly that same-sex couples should have the same legal rights as opposite-sex couples. I feared that my marriage would end up in a divorce like my parents', but we remained respectful throughout the entire process. And when we bump into each other now, we can actually embrace when we say hello.

Sometimes, when I look back on it all, I think we became less as individuals because the marriage meant more. But when we put our resentment away and took the garbage out, we danced in the kitchen, adding something new to a recipe that was always traditional. It wasn't the happy ending we were promised as children, but in the end, we were happier.

CONVERSION

The little white Protestant church stood in the middle of the hill tucked away behind a modest house and some trees. It wasn't as pronounced as its Catholic rival, positioned front and center just down the street. The name, a remnant of its Methodist roots, was a sign that pointed towards the past. Perhaps it's more traditional than other United churches in the city, I thought to myself. But I took a leap of faith and chose to enter anyway.

My friend sang in the church choir. During dinner with him one evening, I told him that my call to ministry never went away.

"The United Church is supportive of gay and lesbian ministers," he said. "You should come with me this Sunday to a service."

I never left the Catholic Church because a priest sexually

abused me. And even when sexual abuse allegations began surfacing in the late eighties, instead of giving up on the church altogether, I considered joining a religious order. I heeded the words of my maternal grandmother: "God got nothing to do with any of that."

And even though I identified as a lesbian, my sexuality wasn't relevant per se because I'd have to be celibate. But my gender couldn't change, or so I thought then, and that's why I left. Women weren't allowed to become priests.

After a period of deep reflection and prayer, I came to the conclusion that I couldn't be a nun because, in my heart, I wanted to be a priest. I've always felt a strong sense of social responsibility, which would've aligned with the charitable work of nuns, but I also wanted to be up where all the action was, on the altar saying Mass.

Being Catholic wasn't just woven into the moral fabric of my being, it was also a huge part of my cultural identity due to my family's deep Irish roots. When my ancestors left the old country in search of a better life, having endured many hardships, Catholicism provided them with an avenue to stay connected to Ireland.

Every year during Easter, my paternal grandfather took me on a tour of various food banks in and around the city. The tour would always begin with us picking up non-perishable food items at the grocery store and then end at the Basilica. He didn't make a lot of money, but this was like an investment to him because he was doing it with me. Back then, people could access churches whenever they needed. Their doors were always unlocked.

Entering the Basilica for the first time will be forever

etched in my memory. As one of the largest construction projects in Newfoundland, and one of the largest church structures in all of North America, sinners have no other choice but to beware. Even the very location of this massive fortress stands contra to the so-called liturgically correct east-west alignment as it faces The Narrows of St. John's harbour, patrolling the sinful citizens of a city named after a saint. Touting itself above its challengers, its hefty presence asserts that to worship God elsewhere is, in fact, a sin. That day, as I placed my tiny foot on the concrete step at its enormous base, I remember feeling smaller than I actually was, and I, a mere child at the time, felt penitent for my sins. But looking back now, I can't help but wonder what exactly did I have to feel sorry for at that age?

Inside, the décor was so ostentatious it made me want to apologize for even being there. The stagnant musky scent—a mixture of hoary incense, mossy stone, and polished wood—hit me like a perfume. The altar in the distance seemed like a mirage, a golden, dangling pendant too heavy to wear. I was seduced by the glamour of it all. It was as if I had been invited into a rich person's home or, as my maternal grandmother would say whenever we walked down Circular Road, a merchant's house. *Jesus could fix everything because he was a carpenter like my uncle*, I kept thinking, and somehow that made me feel like I had permission to be there even though I came from a working-class family. I took my grandfather's hand as we ventured down the aisle. The sunlight piercing the stained glass exposed the tiny dust particles falling through the air like snowflakes.

"One day when you're a bride, your father will walk you

down the aisle," he whispered.

I felt my stomach turn. I dreaded the idea of being a bride. I was seven and had recently had my First Holy Communion. My mother made me wear a dress, and to make matters worse, my teacher forced me to walk down the aisle with a boy who often taunted me in the schoolyard because I wore glasses. When I told my teacher I didn't want to walk with him because of how much he teased me, she told me that when a little boy likes a little girl, he picks on her. And that confused me.

"Miss, if someone likes you, why would they torment you?"

"Boys will be boys," she responded, as she ushered me over towards him.

Boys will be boys—a phrase I often heard when I was young because of how often I asked for help to keep them away from me. As if being a boy was an excuse to behave badly. I had no idea what gender equality meant at the time, but I knew what I was being told was complete and utter bullshit. In that particular moment, however, it wasn't a fight I could win, so I chose to accept my fate and walked down the aisle with a bully: he in his comely grey suit and tie and me in my delicate white dress and veil, looking like a miniature married couple, our union consecrated by our individual sin. We couldn't help but be sinners, according to the church. Our iniquitous ways were mapped out for us the day we were conceived.

– – – – –

Irish migrations to Newfoundland were seasonal at first. English merchants who controlled the commercial fishery hired young men from Ireland. Eventually women joined, and some married the men and stayed on the island, which resulted in the first Irish settlements in Newfoundland. By the mid-1800s, Irish settlers made up half of the province's population.

"Our ancestors had to be like the rock they lived on," my paternal grandmother told me. "Strong enough to withstand the harsh climate and stomach their English masters."

Preserving their religious beliefs in the face of English Protestantism wasn't just about faith, according to my grandmother; it was a form of protest. Even though priests visited the island with European explorers as early as the 1600s, it was 1784 before Pope Pius VI claimed Newfoundland as an ecclesiastical territory, thus altering the cultural topography forever. The growing spiritual needs of the Irish population scattered across the Avalon Peninsula—coupled with the harassment that Catholics endured under British rule through fines, restrictions, and deportation—made the political climate ripe for change.

The appointment of Irish Bishop James Louis O'Donel as the first bishop, in 1796, further solidified the ties between Newfoundland and Ireland, but it wasn't until the appointment of another Irish immigrant, Bishop Michael Anthony Fleming, in 1829, that the church began to build on its foundational missionary work with the construction of a cathedral (which would later be named the Basilica of St. John the Baptist) and establishing parishes. In order to aid in the schooling of a rising population, Fleming welcomed the Presentation Sisters, the Sisters of Mercy, and the Christian Brothers from Ireland to help with education in

Newfoundland, though the Christian Brothers didn't come until later. Under Fleming, denominational education was implemented in 1843, which meant Catholics and Protestants attended separate schools.

Because I was raised Catholic, I grew up thinking I was better than everyone else. Any reference to the past among my eldest family members was filled with tales of how Catholics were exploited by Protestants. And I remember hearing terrible stories of how women were cut off from their families because they ran away with Protestant men.

In primary school, there was a little boy in my class who wasn't Catholic. I'm not sure how he ended up at our school, but he seemed nice enough. Sometimes at recess, he would come over and talk to me. And maybe a small part of me wanted to run away with him, but only as far as the cafeteria so I could get a look at his sister, who was ahead of us by two grades. Whenever my class would go to church, which was conveniently right next door to the school, just down from the convent and below the presbytery, the teacher would seat him in the last pew next to his sister and no one else. They weren't allowed to receive communion. I honestly wished I could be like them because the Body of Christ would get stuck to the roof of my mouth every single time. The first time I tried to pry it off with my tongue, I got in trouble with my teacher because she thought I was chewing gum in church. After that happened, I would just go back to my pew, kneel down, and pretend to pray while I waited for the Body of Christ to disintegrate. Eating unleavened bread in the form of a wafer was like eating cardboard. It wasn't at all appetizing, but perhaps that was the point.

I remembered that boy and girl, who seemed to be internally exiled at church, because my presence at the United Church started creating quite a stir, according to the ministers. Complaints ushered in from a significant portion of the congregation. I was told that some members were uncomfortable with the way I dressed because the clothes I chose to wear were masculine in appearance and I was a female. Others equated being gay with pedophilia and actually thought I would harm the youth in some way. And still others believed that, because I was an out lesbian, I would influence the youth and "turn them." But what hurt the most was during the Passing of The Peace—the equivalent to the Catholic's Peace Be with You, where everyone takes a moment to shake hands—people would literally keep their backs turned to me. That's why I always extend my hand to someone in any situation, even if they're hateful towards me or have hurt me in some way. I know how it feels to be on the other side.

I had been exposed to these types of narrow-minded views before as an activist with a profile, but when you receive threatening phone calls and see damage done to your property, you become somewhat accustomed to such slurs. It may make your blood boil, but it also makes your skin thicken. Beneath that reptilian surface, however, I was hurting. I had left my home church—because, as a "woman," I couldn't be what I wanted to be—only to be rejected by another church due to the fact that I wanted to be *with* a woman. I wasn't sure which church was worse—one that isn't open or one that claims to be. It was a tie. They both lost in the end, because I left.

A common claim of religious fundamentalists is that gays and lesbians have the power to change the sexuality of young people from heterosexual to homosexual, but nothing could be further from the truth. I mean I like to think I'm charismatic, but to believe I could influence young people in this way is preposterous. Throughout the course of my life, however, there have been times when certain people have empowered me to be myself. Their sexual orientation had nothing to do with it. Therein lies the difference. It's not about changing people; it's about empowering them to be themselves.

At a gay bar one evening, in between dances, it was my turn to buy a round for my friends. A young man approached while I was leaning against the bar. He smiled and put his hand on mine, offering to buy me a drink.

"I'm not sure if you remember me," he said, "but I was in your youth group at church. I'm gay, and I just came out to my mother. You have no idea how much you changed my life."

"And you have no idea how much you just changed mine," I responded as I wrapped my arms around him.

We held on to one another for an entire Gloria Gaynor song and cried as hard as we sang. We will survive indeed. If there ever was such a thing as the Church of Gay, that was as close to a religious experience as it gets. There were men in robes, but instead of priests, we called them drag queens. Their perfume was like incense that hung on the air. And when they preached the gospel of love, we said Amen.

As I danced the rest of that night away with my friends, I remember spinning in the middle of the dance floor and watching the lights switch from blue to green to red when, all of a sudden, a light switched on in my head. I had the closure I needed to let that church go because I finally figured out why I was there in the first place.

I felt the presence of God in a gay bar more than any church I've ever been in. Everyone was welcome, and no one was ever turned away. Because we knew what that felt like.

Two years later, a young girl approached me in the Avalon Mall. She looked familiar, but I couldn't place her until she told me that she, too, was a member of the church youth group that I led.

"I hoped to bump into you someday," she said. "This is my girlfriend, Sarah."

And eight years later, at an art gallery, another young person from the youth group approached me.

"Thanks for all your advocacy work," he said. "I look different now than I did when I was in the youth group because I'm trans and on testosterone."

If we have the power to change a person's sexuality, then how could my two incredibly straight parents raise a child who was so different? Our parents are the most influential people in our lives, and my mother and father fit every heterosexual stereotype imaginable. My mother is conventionally beautiful. The way she moves through the world, her speech, her gestures, and her style—from the clothes she wears right down to her accessories—embodies femininity. My father wore suits to work, carried a briefcase, and his shoes were always shined. A star athlete in his day, he still shadow boxes in the mirror and never misses a boxing match, hockey, or baseball game on television. Despite all of that, neither of them impressed their inherent straightness on me. But that's not how sexuality works; though, the irony does prompt a little chuckle every now and then. But thank God I attended that United Church. I threw myself into advocacy work because I never wanted a young person to feel as I did—to want to die because they were different. And I'm happy to report they are all living well, and we remain in touch.

Though the United Church of Canada began to consider the idea of gay and lesbian ministers in the early eighties, it would be a decade later before a gay minister was actually ordained. The membership of the entire church declined as a result. And it was during the nineties that the church also considered same-sex unions, even though same-sex marriage wasn't legal at the time. Almost two decades later, when same-sex marriage was mainstreamed in Canadian culture, the issue caused more rifts within individual congregations, and membership fell once again.

I wished the United Church minister hadn't told me what some of his congregation thought when I first started to attend the church, but he didn't want me to be caught off guard if one of them approached me.

"I've never experienced anything like this," he said with his head down. "I'm so sorry for all of it."

On one occasion, when the service ended, the minister informed everyone that there was a social afterwards and that "All were welcome." Once my friend was done changing out of his choir robe in the backroom, we headed downstairs. There were two ministers at the church, one male and one female. I thought that was encouraging. The female minister was fairly young and a townie, and she was in charge of the youth ministry. She left the service with the children part way through. She eagerly approached us as soon as we entered the church hall. After my friend introduced us, he told her I was interested in becoming a minister. She welcomed me with open arms and encouraged me to get more involved. The demeanour of the male minister, a much older gentleman from Ontario, was soft, unlike his firm handshake. He'd be harder to win over, I thought to myself. If he didn't see me on television lobbying for gay rights, I'm sure he could tell I was a lesbian just by the way I looked. And he would later tell me that he was reserved because he was worried how the congregation would respond.

When I started attending that church, I did what I always do: I rolled up my sleeves and got to work. I volunteered on various church committees, led the youth group, and even became a member of the Church Council. I decided to get confirmed shortly after. The process was different than my confirmation within the Catholic Church.

My parents attended my Catholic Confirmation, and I was seated between them. I remember how awkward it felt because they hardly ever spoke once their divorce was finalized. The archbishop—none other than Alphonsus Penney—was unable to attend, so he sent his second in command, the vicar general.

At the time, learning about the sacraments was part of our curriculum because the school system was still denominational. We said prayers at the beginning of class each morning, before we went to the cafeteria for lunch, and at the end of the day. Always in unison, our principal, who recited them over the PA system, led prayers. We also had to attend Mass regularly throughout the school year. This was consistent throughout primary, elementary, junior high, and high school. Except, in high school, two of my friends were on the student council, so when the weather was actually warm, we'd hide in the student-council room until everyone else was in church then use the exit through the side of the building to access our cars and head to Sunshine Camp for a swim. Though I must admit, the high school I attended was run by Jesuits, and I much preferred the way they said Mass. It felt much more communal.

For our confirmation, our teacher told us that the celebrant would wear the colour red to symbolize the tongues of fire that hovered over the heads of the apostles during Pentecost. No one even batted an eye at that. That was the kind of language we'd grown accustomed to.

When I approached the vicar general, he anointed my forehead, making the Sign of the Cross with consecrated oil, known as the oil of the Chrism. I didn't take a confirmation name, so he said, "Gemma, be sealed with the gift of the Holy Spirit," to which I responded, "Amen." At thirteen, I was viewed as an adult within the eyes of the church.

The United Church accepted my baptism, but in order to become a member, I had to get confirmed.

There are only two sacraments in the United Church: Baptism and Communion. Confirmation is an opportunity for people to reaffirm the commitment made during Baptism. It generally occurs around the ages of ten to thirteen, but people of any age can get confirmed. I invited members of my immediate family to the service and invited a friend to lay her hands on me during the process. In the Catholic Church, Confirmation is one of seven sacraments and is one of the three sacraments of initiation into the church, in addition to Baptism and First Holy Communion. I found the United Church more relaxed in every aspect of worship, except when it came to people who opposed my very presence.

Then when my partner and I started planning our wedding immediately after our engagement, we felt a church wedding wouldn't be an option for us, even though we both identified as Christians. But because we were both activists, we made a decision to apply to be married at all the local United Churches anyway. We knew that would start the process for those churches to consider offering same-sex marriages. I wasn't entirely confident it would work, but I also wasn't prepared for how hard the rejection would hit me. It was difficult to sit in the pew and listen to people pray and sing songs about being kind to others when some members of the congregation were so unkind and unloving towards me.

The process of engaging the church community consisted of holding workshops in order to promote education and encourage dialogue on the topic of same-sex marriage. When the workshops commenced, a congregational vote took place. Before the vote, some members stood up and compared homosexuality to bestiality and pedophilia. I had brought some friends of mine with me for support, and they left part way through because they were so disgusted with the things some of the congregants were uttering. Later, a longstanding member of the congregation told me that even people who weren't members at that church were brought in to sway the vote. The ministers decided not to have a second workshop because the first one went so horribly.

At the church council meeting held to approve the congregational vote that would ensure same-sex blessings would not be performed at the church, I was the only member to abstain. The other members were reluctant to vote against the motion, but felt the congregation had spoken.

Same-sex marriage was legalized in Newfoundland and Labrador on December 23, 2004. As president of Egale Canada, I was involved with other court cases in different provinces, but in my home province of Newfoundland and Labrador, I spearheaded the court case. And the following day, when I walked into the service on Christmas Eve, my head was held high and my hand, as always, was extended. And when I did leave the United Church, I kept in touch with some members who were wonderful while I was there. I am still grateful for their presence in my life during that challenging time.

My partner and I were married at the Bowring Park Bungalow. Hundreds of friends and family gathered in support of our union. But the process of applying for a church wedding and being rejected took an emotional toll on us both. Our marriage eventually ended in divorce, for a number of reasons, but the additional layer of constant societal homophobia didn't help.

But it wasn't all bad. The ceremony and reception were filled with love. My maternal grandmother, who was in her late eighties at the time, sat in the front row during our vows, and she turned to my aunt with tears in her eyes and said, "Love is the same everywhere." She made our wedding cake, too. In fact, she offered to do it without being asked.

"I makes all the wedding cakes for my youngsters and their youngsters," she stated.

"Better be a fruit cake," I winked. And we both laughed.

REMAPPING

I crept down over the stairs and perched on the bottom step waiting for my father to notice me. His back stooped over a dark wooden desk tucked neatly into a corner at the far end of his study. It was early morning. The chirp of birds outside the window muted the harsh stroke of my father's fountain pen as it massacred the papers of his students. Cigarette smoke loitered in the air. Joe Cocker lay on top of the record player flexing without any help from his friends. Books by theologians such as Raymond E. Brown and Hans Kung were posturing over the birth of the Messiah and the existence of God between the couch cushions. When my eyes skipped to the coffee table, I spotted a little black book I hadn't seen before. I jumped up from the stairs and headed towards it. The book, encased in black leather, was small enough to fit into a shirt pocket. On the front in small gold lettering was written, *Twenty-Four Hours a Day*.

"Dad, what does this book mean," I asked.

"I'll tell you about it when you're older," he said.

When my mother and father separated, they both moved back in with their parents. They had joint custody, so I rotated between houses. It wasn't an ideal situation because I was the one always moving around, but it came in handy when one of them got mad at me. I learned how to take advantage of Catholic guilt by the age of four and played them off one another until my late teens.

"Dad, Mom told me I can't watch television after eight o'clock," I whined.

"Put your mother on the phone, please."

"Mom, Dad grounded me again because I was late getting home," I confessed.

"Put your father on the phone, please."

Because both my parents were the first to get divorced in their families, all of my aunts and uncles and both sets of grandparents felt guilty too. My cousin asked his father why I got an extra scoop of ice cream, and my uncle told him it was because my parents got a divorce. I figured I owed it to myself to put everyone's bad feelings towards a good cause. I had two of everything. Birthdays and holidays were celebrated twice.

My father was a teacher at a Catholic high school years before Premier Brian Tobin implemented the non-denominational school system. Up until 1997, the church was the ultimate authority when it came to education in Newfoundland and Labrador, but even though Tobin was a Roman Catholic, he recognized that sustaining denominational education was a drain on the economy. And given the number of abuse allegations that surfaced against Christian Brothers and individual priests in the late eighties and early nineties, it was no surprise that when the Liberal government's second referendum on denominational schools was held, a vast majority of Newfoundlanders voted in favour of putting an end to the religious system. Up until that point, however, the church's tight grip on our educations spanned centuries, so my father kept his divorce a secret in fear of losing his job.

In addition to getting a legal divorce, my parents had to get an annulment. In order for the church to issue the official document, my parents, along with their witnesses, had to testify before a tribunal consisting of priests, nuns, and lay people. The tribunal was tasked with figuring out why their marriage failed. The process took months, but was eventually approved, and my parents were allowed to participate in the sacraments again. When my father tried to explain the concept to me, I was confused. I didn't understand how their marriage no longer existed in God's eyes if they had me while they were married. Did that make me an orphan, I wondered.

Many years passed. I got older and, I'd like to think, a little wiser. My father dropped by my office unexpectedly and gave me a book, one I hadn't seen before called *Adult Children of Alcoholics*. When he left, I read the first paragraph where it stated that if I had an alcoholic for a parent I was likely to become one myself. I immediately stopped reading and slammed the book closed. I felt ill. I rushed to the washroom, stared into the antique oval mirror hanging by a thread on the wall above the sink and said to myself, *This is not who I am*.

But despite my determination, it's impossible to deny that our parents have a deep and lasting influence on our lives and behaviour.

Experts say the first five years in a child's development are the most crucial. Children's brains are like sponges because they absorb everything around them. I learned so many things during my first five years, from crawling to walking to relationships failing. Like many toddlers, my first words were *Mama* and *Dada*, since they were the two people I spent the most time with. It wasn't long after I developed the ability to distinguish sounds and touch that I was able to translate their interactions with one another.

My parents fought all the time. Even when I'd plug my ears with my fingers I could still hear them yelling. It only ended when I entered a room. When I was three, I decided I had enough. I stormed into their bedroom and announced that, if they felt like fighting, they should call out to me since I was the only thing that would make them stop. I thought I had a superpower that could change people whenever I showed up.

One of my earliest memories is of the three of us strolling through Bowring Park. I was in the middle, holding their hands tight with all the strength a three year old could muster. One. Two. Three. And they'd lift me in the air.

"I'm like glue," I told them, as I skipped along, pretending for a moment that fairytales were real. Even back then, I knew I was the only thing holding them together.

I also remember the day my father told me that he and

my mother were separating. I was in kindergarten, and he showed up after I got out of school unannounced in his big, dark blue Plymouth Volare. As much as they tried to shelter me from what was actually happening, they never seemed to give me enough credit. I knew something was up because my father was living with his parents, and my mother and I were living with hers.

My father had just started a job as a teacher at a reputable Catholic high school and was on his lunch break. He always had a great sense of style thanks to his two younger sisters, who helped him shop. On that day, he donned a dark blue raglan, a white and black herringbone tweed jacket, a black turtleneck, and grey dress pants sharply creased up the middle of each pant leg. His wavy dark brown hair perfectly poised on his head and his Chelsea Beatle black ankle boots impeccably shined on his feet.

He presented me my first watch. It had a picture of Mickey Mouse on the front and a red leather strap.

"Remember, Gem, things will get better with time," he said to me.

Whenever my father picked me up from school, he made a detour on the way home to The Ship, a well-known watering hole in downtown St. John's. That was our ritual. I'd sit alone in the car checking my watch, hoping he would come back soon. When he came back to the car, he'd always hand me a bag of salt-and-vinegar potato chips.

The moment I realized my marriage had to end I was at The Ship. I wasn't the first writer to have an epiphany there, that's for sure. That pub was one of the hubs of the cultural renaissance in St. John's during the 1970s and also the best place to listen to live music. The decor was dated, but that was part of its charm.

I checked the time on my watch. I remembered what waiting for someone felt like at 3:30 in the afternoon, and thought about my wife, at home alone, who would be waiting until 3:30 in the morning. I asked the bartender to fetch me a bag of salt-and-vinegar chips—still my favourite—and double-checked my watch. It was a Citizen, the first one I bought for myself. I thought about my father and was hit with a sobering realization. Time creates distance, but it doesn't make things better.

I told the bartender I lost my appetite and asked for a glass of water instead. I left my friends on the dance floor without saying goodbye. I said goodbye to my wife not long after.

For many years, I didn't know whose anger I was carrying around. Was it my father's, my mother's, or my own? Later in life, with a few years of therapy under my belt, my therapist unearthed that it was a mishmash of all three. My parents often took shots at one another by venting to me. I was caught in the middle of a windstorm, and it would be years before I figured out how to stand my ground. I wasn't angry with them for getting a divorce. In fact, I thought it brave, considering it was so taboo at the time. But there's no rulebook on how to be a parent or a spouse. And although the Catholic Church attempted to prepare them for marriage through their marriage preparation program, real-world topics like alcoholism weren't covered in the class.

By age twenty, I was an expert. I could've written a self-help book, but was too busy living it at the time. As a teenager, I was a regular at Alateen meetings and, into early adulthood, a frequent visitor at Al-Anon—offshoots of Alcoholics Anonymous. I could tell the difference between a drunk and a dry drunk and spot their behaviour patterns a mile away. I could recite the twelve steps as effortlessly as a Rosary because they were both repetitiously implanted in my brain. Truthfully, I much preferred the Serenity Prayer to the Lord's Prayer. Mostly for its practicality—I mean, if you're going to say a prayer, you may as well be able to apply it to your daily life. Also, it wasn't so flagrantly patriarchal.

I likened AA to a religion as opposed to a self-help group. It saved people. And literally changed their lives. It gave them a sense of belonging and, most of all, a place to go where they would be accepted no matter what. And similar to the seal of the confessional, meetings were confidential. Don't get me wrong, I understand the need for confidentiality under certain circumstances, but I honestly believe that the reason my father and I both tried to hide parts of ourselves— he in relation to his addiction and me in relation to my sexuality—had to do with shame. And in my opinion, it was the Catholic Church that encouraged this type of response. Shame, like guilt, is pointless. Love has lifted me up. Anger has fuelled me. But shame and guilt have kept me stuck and made me repeat the same habitual destructive patterns.

When I learned at a meeting that the founder of Alcoholics Anonymous saw a light that he interpreted as God as he was detoxing from alcohol, I wasn't the least bit surprised. Religion becomes so embedded in our psyche it's no wonder it appears in our subconscious. But at the time, equating alcoholism with a disease was a difficult pill for me to swallow. At the age of twelve, I watched the life drain from my best friend—my paternal grandfather. He died at the age of sixty-three with bowel cancer. And there was no twelve-step group or higher power to cure him of his illness. He spent the last month of his life in the palliative care unit at St. Clare's Hospital, a mere shadow of the man he was.

The weight of expectation is heavy. It'd almost be easier if we didn't have any expectations at all. At birth we're assigned an encoded gender script. We're told how to feel and think and even how to be. And whether these expectations are placed on us by our parents or the religious faith we are raised in or the societal norms that swirl around us, they seem to lose their power once we become aware of the influence.

My marriage ended in divorce, just like my parents'. So perhaps there was a blueprint for the failure of that relationship. It's difficult to say for sure. But I didn't turn to alcohol, and I was beginning to realize that when it came to me, the expectations of the world around me didn't seem to fit. Being female was something I tried on because it was what I happened to be cloaked in, but I never felt comfortable in my own skin. And I was only beginning to understand that I had the power to change that. Instead of being actualized within someone else's framework, I decided to chart a different path. I rejected the map of expectations and learned how to remap myself.

BAGGAGE

The large oak tree leaned into the house like an old lover. I eyed it up and down, then the house. From the ground, it looked like the window to the room she was staying in was roughly ten feet high. *That's doable*, I thought to myself.

I wasn't much of a climber, but I did feel a kinship with Spider-Man in my youth. The first time I tried to climb something I was nine. It was a concrete wall in the churchyard. I wanted to impress a girl who lived close by, and I prayed to Mary the Virgin Mother to see me through. Actually, I had hoped she'd give me a lift. It was her statue that I was trying to climb. And when I fell, I thought I didn't pray hard enough. As it turns out, the Lord does indeed work in mysterious ways, as the old saying goes. During that lesson in humility, the girl I wanted to impress saw that my hand was bleeding and took me home, which back then meant a glass of milk and a cookie. Score.

But this time, the musician I wanted to impress was staying at a place called Friends House, and because she wasn't the only guest, there was a curfew. I was late as usual. The house was a beautifully preserved heritage home located in the university district of Toronto. The Quakers, also commonly referred to as the Society of Jesus or simply Friends, operated it.

Quakers don't participate in a mass or service. They hold a "meeting" instead. It's not a typical meeting. There's no set agenda. Meetings are generally held in silence until someone feels compelled to speak about a spiritual insight or social justice concern often referred to as "ministry." Usually, a person only speaks once because it isn't a place for discussion. At the end of the meeting, announcements are read and everyone shakes hands before heading to the dining area for coffee or tea. Silence, they believe, is what centers a person and brings them back to the inner voice of God, which we all carry within us.

The meetings were held in the back room of Friends House. The first time I attended one, the large wall of windows framed the back garden while a large circle of chairs embraced the room. The décor was modest. I had gotten so used to the opulence of the Catholic Church, the hard wooden pews as outdated as the dogma, that when I first entered a United Church and there was padding, I felt uncomfortable, almost spoiled. The chairs at Friends House, much like those United Church pews, were as welcoming as the room and were filled with a garland of people of all shapes and sizes. Some were staying at the house, and others lived close by. The room wasn't filled with profligate relics dipped in gold because the smiles from the people who greeted you took up the entire space. I felt at ease there.

On this night, after an ardent climb to the top of the tree, I tapped on her window. She threw it open and said, "Oh Gem, I love you for scaling the side of the house, but I did manage to leave the front door unlocked."

I never even checked. In fact, it never crossed my mind at all.

"Why do you always take the longest, most difficult way round?" she joked.

"Makes the prize that much more worthwhile."

She laughed, hauled me into her room, and then into her arms. I didn't get a glass of milk or a cookie, but believe me, I scored.

And that's often how I thought of it back then: as if sex was a game and I was a player, always out to score. I didn't see this woman solely as the spoils of a successful conquest; I had a deep affection for her. Yet the language of objectification and conquest always seemed to obscure or perhaps conceal the language of honest intimacy and emotion.

I can't pinpoint the exact moment in my life when I began to view sex in this way. But I know that, for some time, I was trying to prove myself in male spaces. And when you desperately want to be accepted within a social group, that kind of gendered behaviour can creep in before you realize it. Maybe it had something to do with the way I was trying to impress my male friends with my sexual exploits. Maybe I was simply using sex to bolster my damaged sense of self-worth. Maybe it was a lot of things. But one question remained: why did I so incessantly seek that validation in the company of men? That question kept repeating like the sound of my steps as I beat down the pavement along the Trans-Canada Highway until I finally reflected on another question, one I had avoided all of my life up until now: Do I want to be a man?

The first time I laid eyes on her was at an event in support of women artists in a chic martini bar in downtown St. John's, where we were both asked to perform. She was promoting her second album, and I was reading poems from a manuscript that was nowhere near finished. When she was on stage, she held my gaze the entire time. I just had to have her.

After the show was over, she approached me while I was at the bar.

"Wow, you really know how to command a room," she said. "You could hear a pin drop when you read your poetry."

"You flatter me, but I'll take it," I replied. "I'm just glad I went before you."

She invited me to her gig at The Ship the following night, but there was a storm and snow squalls made the roads unsafe. Not unusual in Newfoundland because the weather is unpredictable. But I knew I would see her the following Sunday. She was performing at a brunch that I was actually helping to plan, though up until the previous Friday, I only knew her by way of reputation.

After she finished performing at the brunch, I approached her and apologized for not making it to The Ship.

"The show did go ahead," she told me. "And I looked for you."

"Well, here's my business card if you're interested in

giving me a private performance." I casually handed her my card and walked away.

Two weeks went by and I hadn't heard from her, so I took matters into my own hands. I found her website and sent her an email.

> Subject: Forecast
> Looks like Friday night could be hot.
> Drink?

One week later, she finally replied. It wasn't like I checked my email every five seconds or looked at the pictures on her website ten times a day or anything. Whatever. I totally did. The fact that she didn't respond immediately intrigued me even more.

> Subject: Re: Forecast
> Too soon to tell what Saturday will look like, but I'm down for a drink.
> Plus, Friday I have a gig. I'd invite you, but I don't want you to rain on my parade.

Whoa. I wasn't expecting such a retort. Were we both playing games now? I remember walking around feeling impaired because her image was the only thing I could see. I couldn't eat or sleep, but I savoured every delectable moment of blissful torment. I suggested we get a drink at the martini bar where we first met. When I arrived, she was sitting on a stool dressed like someone out of a magazine and sipping a glass of whiskey straight up. Her clothes hugged her sculpted figure so perfectly it was as though they were custom made. Around both her wrists were silver bangles that gently jingled whenever her arms moved. I noticed a lone silver ring on her left hand containing a large opal, and on her right was a thick silver band with etched designs. I ordered a drink and suggested we move to the comfy chairs in the back corner.

We talked for hours before heading to a jazz bar where we danced to live music until close. When we left the bar I knew she was trying to decide whether or not to take me home. I took her hand and headed towards the harbour front. The air was crisp, but the sky was clear. Not even the city lights could cast a shadow on the stars. Looking at her I wondered why some stars shine more than others. At one point, we sat on the large rope that tied a ship to the dock. When the ship pulled out slightly, the movement hoisted us up into the air. It was dangerous, but we both knew the risk going in. As soon as we landed, she told me to call a cab.

When I walked into her living room, there were as many instruments on the floor as cushions and not a single chair. We curled up in the corner. She hadn't yet made up her mind if she was taking me upstairs, but I was feeling hopeful because she told me her male partner was out of town for the weekend.

"What would you do if you met you in a dark martini bar, Gemma?"

I pulled her closer to me and gently moved my thumb across her mouth. Her lips had a pinkish hue and were almost heart shaped. Her eyes were the colour of the earth. I wanted to bury myself in them so that I'd be the only thing she'd see. Her eyebrows arched naturally. Nothing about her beauty was deliberate. Turning her gently to one side, I caressed the nape of her neck slowly. Within seconds my hand was plotting a course all along her perfect frame. Before I reached below her waist, she took me by the hand and led me upstairs. She disrobed and placed herself naked before me on her bed. Her elbows prompted her breasts upright, yet it was the cross of her legs that unhinged me. I got down on my knees. Her legs fell open. When I gave her my mouth, her slight body began to lean steadily into its rhythm. I inhaled her scent like a drug. My eyes fixated on her stunning face, ceaselessly swept up by her long ebony coloured hair as her head shifted from left to right. Her hand tugged on my hair as her body jerked.

Afterwards it was as if an electric current surged through my groin when she cradled her guitar naked and sang to me. As I lay there awestruck watching her, I began to trace my finger along the inside of her thigh. When she finished her song, I told her I wanted to write invisible lines of poetry all over her skin.

"No need to brand me," she said. "I'm already yours."

But she was moving back to Nova Scotia for the summer and to Toronto in the fall to attend university.

I would go to her whenever she could see me, but the secrets of twilight seemed to swallow endless possibilities for new lovers with big dreams. She left her partner, but I married someone else.

We lived large while we were together. Always leaving a trail of empty champagne bottles and rose petals in every hotel room. Good thing I tipped well.

At that point in my life, I was only living in the moment. I never thought about the future. When you come close to death, it's difficult to come down off that edge. Parts of my life were so unbearable that I moved from one distraction to another. It worked for a time, but I knew I'd have to make a decision, and after years of therapy I learned how to choose myself.

I caught a glimpse of a future in the face of the woman I married. I saw the family I never had. I clung to the idea of her as if my life depended on it. But no one can be our lifeline. And when we put everything into someone else, we lose ourselves in the process. Eventually, we lose them, too.

— — — — —

Some years had passed. The heat hovered like a Newfoundland fog in Toronto as I stared out the open window of a taxi on my way back to see the musician. I showed up on her doorstep with a red rose and the fragile sticker from my luggage poking out of my shirt pocket. I caught the red eye from St. John's, but she was waiting for me in a silk robe with a wine glass half-full. I drank it half-empty. My marriage had ended. Humour may have been my defense in the past, but at that time, I wasn't trying to be funny.

I undid her robe and fell to my knees. I wept as I pressed my head against her waist. I felt as though I had been lost at sea. I was washed up now. She held my head tight to her and sang to me softly.

She poured herself a bath and me another glass of wine. Once she immersed herself in the water, she handed me the cloth that hung on the side of the old claw-foot tub. After I bathed her, I shaved her legs. We didn't speak. There was no room for words.

We had come a long way, her and I, and found the space to be together again in various cities in between other lovers, but in the end we realized our lives were going in different directions. What we lost as lovers, we gained as friends.

At that time, the Christian heteronormative ideal was the standard I used to measure my self-worth, and I always came up short. I thought that if I could be like everyone else, God would love me. That included being involved in a church community and getting married. There's nothing wrong with those things, but for me, my whole identity was contingent on being accepted. But how do you fit into these constructed roles when you don't know how to fit into your own life or your own body for that matter?

I came to the realization that the way I embodied my physicality impacted how I related sexually to other women, and it didn't just hold me back in relationships: it held me back from myself. All my life, I thought I was living a lie, but as it turns out, I wasn't the one who was lying. The truth is I'm not sinful. Or evil. Or wrong. I'm not defined by my past, nor am I constrained by it.

Maybe the musician was right. I do like to make things harder on myself, but it wasn't easy to let go of the baggage I had been carrying with me all these years. As I walked I couldn't help but notice that I started to feel lighter. Instead of putting my faith in an institution or a person, I decided to start having some faith in myself.

WHITE FLAG

"You mind that scarf now till I see you again," the poet said as she tossed it round my neck.

The cab pulled up and just like that she was gone.

My marriage had recently ended, and an older gay couple, two dear friends of mine, asked me to housesit while they were travelling abroad. I invited the poet over for dinner. At the door, she presented me with a beautiful bottle of Beaujolais with her right hand; her left hand remained hidden behind her back.

"This will do perfectly," I said. And then, joking about the differences in our ages, "I like my wines young and my women..."

"Careful now," she cautioned.

"Aged," I responded with a smirk.

She noted my wit and surprised me with a bouquet of lilacs.

"Lilacs!" I exclaimed.

Our mutual affection for lilacs was revealed during our email courtship. As it turned out, I had collected a modest bunch earlier that day as an ornament for the dinner table. She knew by my reaction that I had some already picked.

"Some hard to surprise the likes of you, Gemma Hickey," she said in a playful tone.

I told her a tall tale of how I risked my life to get them for her. I scavenged the neighbourhood knocking on every door (it was one door) to see if anyone had them in their yard. One woman took pity on me because it was raining hard (gently sprinkling) and let me dry off in her porch (she had to answer the phone and told me to wait inside). She directed me to a lilac tree next to the old Grace Hospital. As I arrived in the parking lot, I slipped on the mud (tripped up in myself because I wasn't paying attention) and fell down a hill (a slight bump in the gravel). And when I finally made it to the tree, I broke a branch (more like a twig) as I climbed and fell down the tree (that was actually true) but was able to clutch a handful of lilacs as I fell (also true).

"Impressive," she admitted. "But I risked my mortal soul."

We were both raised Catholic. She won.

Apparently she snuck into the yard of a convent and stole lilacs from the tree when the nuns weren't looking. I took out a bigger vase and placed hers and mine together. The house was filled with the scent of lilacs for days.

When we sat down to eat, we barely touched our food. The conversation was too delicious. Over dinner she told me she couldn't see me for two months because she had an old lover coming for the summer.

"Will she let you have a younger lover," I asked.

"She's French and very jealous," she warned.

I lay beside her scarf that night in bed. Her first book of poems folded on my bare chest, the thin pages gently tickled my skin like the lashes of her eyes earlier that evening. I knew she wouldn't give herself over to me easily. Her heart was like the old country—a place I've never been, but have always longed for. Before nodding off, I devised a plan to conquer it.

It all started when she invited me over to her house for dinner.

"Bring some of your poems and a bottle of red," she insisted.

I was full of nerves as I stood on her doorstep. She was my favourite Newfoundland poet after all. I held the large yellow envelope containing my poems tightly in hand. Just as she opened the front door, a flock of seagulls set sail in the sky above us. Our heads lifted instantly.

"Their wings are like the sails of The White Fleet," she said.

Newfoundlanders often called the Portuguese fishing fleet The White Fleet because of the white sails that adorned their vessels. Due to the length of the fishing season, which lasted six months, ships would frequently dock in St. John's harbor in need of supplies or safety. For decades, Portuguese fishermen could often be seen playing soccer along the waterfront or shopping for souvenirs in the downtown area. Long before the federal government comprised of so-called Progressive Conservatives imposed the Cod Moratorium in 1992, codfish were bounteous in Newfoundland waters.

The fishing industry bolstered the economies of both Portugal and Newfoundland. Other countries exploited the fishery, including the one we joined in 1949, but the relationship between Portugal and Newfoundland was unique. It was sacrosanct. In 1955, a celebration in St. John's marked five hundred years since the King of Portugal claimed the Grand Banks as Terra Nova. It ended with roughly four thousand Portuguese fishermen marching to the Basilica in St. John's, some of them carrying a statue of Our Lady of Fatima, which was presented to the archbishop by the priest from the fleet, symbolizing the affable exchange between the two cultures. Some of Newfoundland's earliest settlements still bear the names assigned by Portuguese explorers.

What I discovered in history class, the poet experienced firsthand. She made friends with many of the fisherman and visited Portugal often. She had the pictures on her wall to prove it. Her poetry was even translated into Portuguese. So it wasn't a coincidence that I chose a red wine from Portugal when I visited the liquor store earlier that day. She noticed it right away as I handed the bottle to her in her porch, even though a straggly little black dog kept yapping at our feet.

Entering her living room was like being transported to another world. It had the ambiance of a speakeasy from the 1940s with a Newfoundland accent. Silk scarves from France hung like drapes over the table lamps, and the walls, painted in earthy greens, were decorated in art that was as eclectic as her music collection. The scarlet drapes enclosed the plants that lined the window ledge like a stage curtain—their blooms almost garnered applause they were so impressive. The wood stove was the centerpiece of the room, the envy of the old coal fireplace, which was off to one side. Handily located across from the couch, the woodstove was bright red with a gold trim. Newspapers were stacked at its base as if spring was yesterday's news.

The furniture was largely comprised of antiques. An old wooden table was used as a desk—once a fisherman's culling board to sort dried and salted cod. I imagined if I laid my head down on it I could almost hear the hush of the fish—the death of an industry. Blade marks more plentiful than wood grains. Appropriate that the taste of salt is more bitter than sweet, an echo of waves on the shore of our province's memory. On top of the desk was a pair of reading glasses and a stack of papers stuffed with words. Bookshelves, over-flowing with books, lined most of the walls as well as the coffee table. Pieces of driftwood relaxed in front of a long line of picture frames on whatever surface remained—artifacts of a life well-travelled.

Her kitchen resembled a European café. Walls of bright yellow and red were kept in line by a navy trim. Cookbooks ruled an entire wall, while a poster from an old theatre troupe, postcards from Portugal, and images of Irish writers Samuel Beckett and William Butler Yeats had no point of order. More plants decorated each of the three window ledges, and strings of white lights were draped over the top of two windows. Long white candles in a brass candelabrum sealed a faded floral tablecloth with wax drippings. Her daughter was seated at the table beside her partner. I joined them once we were introduced. The kitchen was tight, but the poet knew her way around it. Once a dancer, it was as if hermovements were choreographed. Every now and then I'd catch a glimpse of her twirling around the chairs, shaking herbs in a jar filled with garlic, olive oil, and balsamic vinegar. She didn't miss a beat, but my heart may have skipped a few.

A superb meal and four bottles of wine later, she was teaching me how to tango in her living room. After some practice, I was actually starting to get the hang of it until I lost my balance and we toppled over and on to the floor. We were laughing so loud when we landed that her daughter, who was trying to sleep in the room directly above us, thudded on the floor with her foot. We playfully tiptoed to the couch. Once we were seated, she asked me to hand her the envelope containing my poems. I wanted to watch her as she read me, but I looked away instead and pretended not to care. Inside, my heart was racing. Her approval meant everything to me.

She paused before reading each poem. Then read them again.

"You've got the rhythm down," she said.

Phew, I thought to myself.

"Read this one to me," she insisted.

I became shy all of a sudden, but felt relieved when she closed her eyes.

SOUVENIR
(With apologies to Neruda)

I do not love you as if you were a souvenir
We have not travelled that far

The blankets of years do not weigh on us
In a proverbial bed

There are not enough things between us
To lock the doors

(My house is empty and yours is full)

I love you, as you ought to be loved
When the curtains are closed

I love you with the intention of words
And the guts of skin

I love you though I cannot have you
Still, I would go to you

I would blanket you with my arms and mouth
And lift you up in a bed of verse

And when you leave
I will be your souvenir

"Put that one in your book," she ordered.

Her eyes were still closed. Mine were blinded by wine and poetry. Nothing was clear, so I set my sights on her. I moved in closer and kissed her lips gently. Her hands, no longer resting clumsily on her lap, turned fresh and took hold of me. Until suddenly, without warning, they closed as if I were a book that she decided not to finish. She had read me enough to know that she had been that poem before.

"Time for you to go home out of it," she said. "I'll call you a cab."

"I'll wait outside," I said.

"Will you let me know you got home okay," she asked.

"Sure, you're not me fuckin' girlfriend," I saucily replied, for a laugh.

She'll have me back, I thought to myself. I told the cabbie to take me to Lime Street. A good friend of mine, also a writer, was on deadline, so I knew she'd still be up. I staggered through her front door and sat down at her kitchen table. She poured us both a shot of Jamesons as I recounted the evening.

"You gotta start writing this shit down," she told me.

"Good idea," I said. "Hand me a pen."

I got up from the table carefully, swiped a napkin from the counter, and headed for the couch. I decided I should write the poet a little letter stating my case. I placed the napkin on my knee and somehow managed to jot this down:

> *Dearest Poet,*
>
> *You can't be a girl's favourite poet, invite her over for a candlelit dinner, get her drunk on fine wines, ask her to tango in your living room, and not expect to be kissed.*
>
> *That is all.*
>
> *Yours,*
> *Gemma*

I awoke to a terrible headache; the napkin was crumpled up in my hand. I opened it up and laughed at what I read. I loved that she kicked me out of her house at three in the morning. It made me want her even more. I lay there for a little while longer, replaying the night over in my head. I checked my phone before going to the washroom and was pleasantly surprised when I opened my email to find one from her:

> *Wonderful to be in your company, saucy as you are.*
> *Until we meet again, which I hope is soon.*
> *Nice dancer, by the way.*

I was in.

I devised a plan the moment she told me of her reunion with the French lover. Determined to make her mine, I sought the help of her daughter to let me in her house. I pruned and strategically positioned sixty-two long-stem red roses in glass vases in each room and on the card I wrote:

Sixty-two red roses—one for each day of July and one for each day of August. So you don't forget how fabulous I am and you don't forget how fabulous I think you are.

Gemma

Later that day I received an email from her, and in true poetic fashion she wrote, "Holy Fuck."

The French lover did indeed come, but not for very long. We spent a feverish summer together. Floating while on fire. Each day was an enchanting paradox of physical calm and high elation. We collapsed habitually in pitches of clover. We watched clouds spool, and hid in grassy knolls eaves-dropping on waves. We foraged for food along river streams. Cooked together. Laughed often. Drank fine wines and danced. Bathed naked in saltwater as whales pirouetted around the cape in arched curves. I read to her most nights as she lay in my arms. Her breath on my chest made me face each day with solidity.

"Look at me," she'd whisper to me when we made love. "It doesn't have to be a performance."

Uh-oh, I thought to myself.

Suddenly, thanks to this woman's incredible powers of perception and insight, I was revealed. It was a performance, and I liked to think I was good at it. I was welcomed in male spaces as a result of my sexual exploits with women, and I was the envy of some of my male friends because, as a woman, I was accepted in female spaces too, like an informant or double agent. Upon reflection, my superficial bravado, an intolerable form of masculinity, became my disguise, my armour. Did society condition men to be this way, I wondered? Was I trying to be like a man? There were more questions than answers. For some reason I needed affirmation from women to feel good about myself because my ego was so fragile. It occurred to me that it wasn't my homosexuality that was premature as my conversion therapist implied; it was my sexuality in general. I was sexualized at a young age, too young, and so through adolescence and adulthood, I ended up over sexualizing my relationships with others.

Of course, there were times when I felt love for people and I had the best intentions when getting involved, but one thing became clear to me as I walked and reflected along that long stretch of highway—sex, for me, had been about conquest: conquest in the name of boosting my sense of self-worth, while avoiding or concealing the underlying self-doubt and self-loathing. I came to the conclusion that when you've been sexually violated early on, it's difficult to be in your body when allowing someone else to enter that same space. Always the narrative played in my head like a depressing song on repeat: *This person will hurt you. You're ugly. You're unlovable. You're nothing. Who do you think you are? You don't deserve this.*

But I dropped the performance, and our intimate life

became more like a slow waltz. I raised my white flag and it became a white sail. I followed her lead with eyes wide open.

We lived together for a time, and it was blissful, that is until reality set in. She was of another generation and became preoccupied with the difference in our ages.

"I don't ever want to be a burden on you," she said.

"Don't be so foolish," I responded. "I can't wait to spend the money I'm going to save with your senior-citizen discounts."

"Gemma, your humour saves me every time," she said as the laughter bellowed out of her.

Age difference aside, what made cohabitating even more impossible was that she liked to spend long periods of time in solitude.

"I prefer my own company mostly," she'd warn.

Even when we'd go for long walks together she insisted on walking ahead of me.

"I like walking alone," she'd remind me.

I could never catch up to her because she was always a step ahead. Her push was as strong as her pull, and eventually the tug on my heart gave way.

"I fear that my arms are too small for a heart the size of yours," she said. "Perhaps I'm too set in my ways."

— — — — —

The endless miles of solitude along the Trans-Canada were allowing me insight, not only about the poet, but about myself, too. Our romance was a whirlwind, but in between the waves of emotion, we had great discussions on New-foundland nationalism, literature, and jazz. She often talked about how colonialism infiltrated the most sacred of spaces and how the media influenced the way we embody our sexuality. She never wanted to be categorized, and I admired how she was always trying to feel her way through life and not live it according to some prescribed way of being. She challenged me on every level. The mixture of fragility and strength I experienced during my time with her made me realize that I can be emotionally present in a relationship. And though we didn't last as lovers, I knew we would eventually become friends.

"I love your memory even though I know it's hard on you," she said, "but it's what makes you a writer. Promise when you write me you won't forget that I loved you," she said.

One crisp day, when I was making good time on my walk, I decided to break early. I found a guardrail to sit on. Took a sip of Gatorade and ate a protein bar. Every day I'd pack a book of poetry in my backpack, and today I carried the collected works of Elizabeth Bishop. She was heavier than I anticipated, but I was becoming stronger as the days passed. Spending that kind of time alone will do that to you. You have to dig deep and ignore the physical pain. Mind over matter. I could feel a shift within me as I walked. The poet was right about solitude. I too was beginning to enjoy my own company.

At the bottom of my backpack was a pen the poet brought back to me from Portugal in honour of my thirty-fourth birthday. I opened my notebook and, using my knee like a desktop, began to write:

AT THE BOOKSTORE

After the play I walked you as far as Prescott Street,
but had to stop myself there.
Everything hurts, I said.

You turned to me with tears in your eyes
and I wiped them away.
I cupped your face with both my hands,
kissed your forehead, then your lips.
You fixed my collar
and noted that the shirt was new.

Why do you have to be stubborn? I asked.
One of us has to be, you said with a smile.

I watched you walk away then.
You turned round once.

It's easier to look back
from a distance.

At the bookstore they took
five bucks off Elizabeth Bishop.
The clerk said she was damaged.
Most of us are, I told him.

HOPE WALK:
ARNOLD'S COVE TO HOLYROOD

DAY 29

I had fallen behind again, but only slightly. The weather was operatic—the wind conducted the rain, and together they struck me from all directions as I walked forty-two kilometers without rest. The lights flashing from the RCMP escort following devotedly behind me cut through the fog and served as a warning for oncoming traffic. My face was wind burnt, blisters covered my lips, and just like the weather, my insides were chaos.

> Facebook Post: "Day 29 and it's my worst day yet in terms of the weather. Rain and wind pounding hard and lots of fog. But thankfully I have an RCMP escort following behind me. And I don't think I'm going to get a ticket for speeding."

I was also on my period, and with each step, the cramps in my stomach amplified.

I first started having my period when I was eleven years old. And every twenty-eight days, it would feel like my insides were imploding. Like clockwork, two weeks before my period would start, I'd experience PMS (premenstrual syndrome) in the form of depression and anxiety, and a week before, I'd have insomnia and diarrhea in addition to food cravings, fluid retention, and body aches. When my period would start, the cramps were so debilitating I'd have to take sick days from school and work. I tried regular painkillers like acetaminophen and ibuprofen, but they didn't work, nor did the naproxen my doctor prescribed. At twenty-two, I begged him to sign off on a hysterectomy, but he refused.

"It may seem like suffering now, but wait until you bring a baby into the world," he said.

I never, ever had a desire to give birth, even though I love children dearly. I just wanted the pain and discomfort to end, and I knew my mother had problems for most of her adult life when it came to her menstrual cycle. I remember seeing her buckled over in pain when I was four and kneeling down at her bedside to pray because I thought she was going to die. When I asked my grandmother why my mother was so ill, she told me that every month this happens to women because Eve made Adam eat an apple.

I always loved a good story, but the talking snake seemed to be a bit of a stretch on top of everything else. Besides, I was told apples were good for you. Already I was seeing contradictions. And later when I was studying Abrahamic religions in university, which were male-centric, I began to put the puzzle pieces together.

At thirty-two, the PMS I was experiencing was even more

intense and my periods still excruciatingly painful. I had a new doctor and she was more sympathetic, but she wouldn't sign off on a hysterectomy because I wasn't over the age of forty. She did, however, refer me to see a gynecologist who gave me the option of either an IUD (intrauterine device) or the birth-control pill to offset my PMS and prevent me from menstruating. I never liked using tampons, so didn't find the idea of having a device implanted inside me very appealing. I opted for birth-control pills instead, but decided to stop taking them after a year because I gained weight and my mood swings worsened. Estrogen and I never agreed with one another, and I was finally beginning to understand why.

DAY 30

Before Clayton dropped me off on the highway, I sat in the truck to do an interview with Fred Hutton on VOCM. The truck was parked in front of the trailer at BlueFin RV Park in Holyrood. It was overcast and cool, and I was ready to take on the day after a solid night's sleep. I literally fell into my bed the night before having walked forty-two kilometers straight.

I chose to walk the highway instead of the old railway bed for the sake of visibility. The highway was more interactive due to traffic, whereas the railway bed, though the distance was shorter, went from one community to another with nothing in between but woods. I wanted to raise awareness and funds for Pathways, and on the highway, people could actually see that I was doing what I set out to do.

Throughout the course of the walk, I'd make posts on social media and every couple of days do a short video where

I'd talk into the camera of my phone as I walked in order to engage my followers and give them a snapshot of me with the highway as my backdrop. They were also a useful fundraising tool to promote the Pathways website. The video I took on Day 30 was to promote the finale and some local downtown businesses in an effort to get people to visit them. The Club offered the Gemma burger; Rocket Bakery, the cookie; Fogtown, the haircut; and YellowBelly, the beer. Other businesses like The Sprout offered specials. The proceeds from their sales went towards Pathways, and I was so moved by all of the support I was receiving.

> Facebook video: "Two days away from the big finale on August 2, 4 p.m. at the Mount Cashel Memorial. And you know one of the things I love, one of the many things I love about being out here on the road aside from meeting all of the wonderful people from this province and seeing all of the beautiful landscapes is that I get to eat whatever I want because I've been walking so much every day. I've been carbing it up big time. And today, you too can carb it up."

The excitement of being two days away from St. John's distracted me from the cramps I was still experiencing because of my period. Ryan Cleary, NDP Member of Parliament for St. John's South-Mount Pearl, met me on the highway partway through my first interval and walked with me for ten kilometers. He and I were also working together on a bill for a National Institutional Abuse Awareness Day. And as friends, we laughed often, which kept my spirits high and also distracted me.

Shortly after Ryan left and I was walking alone, the cramps waned a little, but my breasts felt incredibly tender. I could feel them when my arms moved back and forth as I walked.

I only ever noticed my breasts when I was on my period because they would swell and feel sore. Most of the time, I'd wear two sports bras or a binder to keep them hidden. I never felt connected to them. They looked like two growths on my chest. I often thought back to my childhood years when I'd walk around bare chested. I longed for that feeling of freedom again. But I often felt guilty about not wanting my breasts because good friends of mine had lost their breasts to cancer.

And I also remembered seeing a picture of my friend Gerry Rogers, a well-known filmmaker and activist, on the front cover of *The Independent*, a local newspaper, back in 2007. The image of Gerry, bare-chested with her two hands covering the scars from her double mastectomy, was completely drained of colour so it appeared black and white except for the bright red lipstick that adorned her lips. I thought it was the most powerful image of a woman I'd ever seen. Gerry was the epitome of confidence and self-definition. And she helped me feel I could be self-defined as well.

At the end of Day 30 on the road, I decided that when I returned to St. John's I'd not only look into starting hormone therapy, but I'd also explore the possibility of having my breasts removed. And I remembered back to Day 19, when I'd shouted my name into the hills and the echo returned it to me. I knew that even though I would now take steps to transform my body, I was going to keep my name.

DAY 31

I was so close now. Not just to the finish line, but to a new beginning. I never felt like a woman, but when I was young, I didn't have the vocabulary to describe what I was thinking and feeling. My body has changed over the years due to growth spurts, weight loss and gain, and aging. And this was no different, really, because on the inside I was still the same person. I was still Gemma. In a way, I'd been transitioning since the day I was born. I never wanted to erase the person I was because that person informed the person I was becoming. This is what I was thinking as I wet my hair in the bathtub before my haircut.

My barber and friend, Chris Evans, co-owner of Fogtown Barber and Shop, was in British Columbia for a wedding, but he wanted me to look my best for my finale the next day. He sent Dan McCarthy, one of his employees, to our campsite in Holyrood to give me a haircut. Dan told me that Chris gave him specific instructions on how to cut my hair.

"I'm surprised Chris isn't flying back from BC to do this himself," he said. "I feel honoured that he trusted me with you."

We both laughed.

> Facebook Post: "Day 31 begins bright and early!
> Why? Because a barber from Fogtown is driving
> out to my camp to cut my hair for the big finale
> tomorrow. Seriously. How awesome is that!
> Then more walking in the wind and rain, but at
> least I'll look sharp!"

I went to see Chris at his barbershop every week. He was tall and devilishly handsome. Though his short blonde hair was always hidden beneath a Fogtown baseball cap, it was always neatly faded. His blue eyes possessed the wonderment of a child's, and his heart was as open as his demeanor was playful. Like his character, his arms were sturdy, and they were covered in tattoos, which reminded me of my paternal grandfather. I felt comfortable around Chris. We had great chats about life, our family histories, and the future of the province we lived in. I didn't have facial hair for Chris to shave, but he always tapped my face gently with aftershave when he was done. I left his barbershop each week feeling like a king.

Dan did an amazing job with my hair. Having walked for thirty-one days straight, I reveled in feeling fresh again. And I hit the highway with a spring in my step.

After I clocked five kilometers, I raised my hand to signal to the RCMP escort that I wanted to stop. I felt a strong urge to urinate, having had two cups of coffee and a full bottle of Gatorade before leaving camp. I spotted some bushes and made my way towards them. Whenever I needed to stop, the RCMP officer would exit his vehicle and stand on guard on the highway shoulder. His hands were on his hips and his eyes peeled on the highway. It made me feel important.

> Facebook Post: "Every time I leave the highway's shoulder, this man stands watch. Thanks RCMP for having my back. Tomorrow as I enter town, the RNC will follow me home."

Well-concealed behind some scraggly spruce trees and bushes, I dropped my pants to finally relieve my poor bladder, and as I was bent down, I got stung on my backside by a stout (known elsewhere as a deer fly). Now, for an insect no larger than a housefly, a stout packs quite a wallop. Not only do the stings hurt, but they become very itchy really quickly.

Back on the road, that bite on my butt cheek became incredibly uncomfortable, but with the RCMP officer diligently following behind me, there was nothing I could do about that itch without embarrassing myself.

So here I was on the final leg of my journey with my heroic return just around the corner, and all I could think about was trying not to scratch my ass.

TIME

Years before my paternal grandfather died, I made a special request. I had walked into his bedroom as he was carefully placing his gold pocket watch in a blue metal tin where he kept some of his personal items and documents. The watch was a treasured possession, a gift from the Canadian National Railway for twenty-five years of service.

"What are you up to, Pop?" I asked.

"Putting my pocket watch away to be given to your cousin Matthew when I die."

Matthew was the youngest grandchild on that side of my family. Because he was a baby, he got more attention from my grandparents than I did, and I didn't like that one bit.

"I want your pocket watch, Pop."

"I was only leaving it to Matthew because he's a boy."

Of course, the passing down of such an heirloom to the eldest male child is a longstanding Western tradition, and my grandfather meant nothing personal by it. But at the time, I was jealous of Matthew because, even though he was much younger than me, he seemed to exist on a higher level in the family hierarchy simply because he was a boy—the first boy.

I was also jealous because the pocket watch meant a great deal to my grandfather; it was a symbolic item owned by a person who meant the world to me.

I remember dipping my tiny hand in the holy-water font by the front door in my great-grandparent's house whenever my grandfather took me there to visit his mother. His father, James, had worked at the railway dockyard, while his mother, Mary, raised ten children in their two-storey home on Barter's Hill. I never met my great-grandfather because he died eighteen years before I was born, but I was fortunate to know my great-grandmother. Her long grey hair was usually tied up in a bun, and she wore stylish dresses, even at home.

The house on Barter's Hill was painted dark green and was attached on both sides. The mature trees in the backyard were always pruned and the grass trimmed, but in the summertime, everyone lounged on the front step and drank the spruce beer that great-grandmother made. In the parlour, the sofa and accent chair were covered in plastic because that room was only used for special occasions. Everyone congregated in the kitchen, the traditional gathering place in most Newfoundland homes. There was a built-in china cabinet and a chrome dining set. My great-grandmother's rocking chair was also chrome. It was next to the daybed by the stove. There was a bottle of liniment in the cabinet that you could inhale to ease a cold, and it could also be rubbed on your skin for muscle aches. The Rosary was said on Sunday evenings after supper, and there was a list of prayers for other nights of the week. Upstairs there were three fully furnished bedrooms and a bathroom.

My great-grandmother died at the age of ninety-four. I was nine years old. My father wrote my teacher a note so I could attend the funeral with my grandparents. After the Mass, all the cars formed a procession to Mount Carmel Cemetery. As her coffin was lowered into the ground, I held my grandfather's hand. I felt confused and scared because it was the first time I had experienced the death of a family member. Seeking some kind of explanation or assurance, I asked my grandfather why people die.

"To be reunited with God in heaven, Gem."

I remember looking around at the hundreds of tombstones and wondering why so much space was being used on earth when heaven was up above us.

In my family, many nights were spent around the kitchen table. Tall tales were swapped like playing cards. Whoever had the best story didn't win a pot of money like in a card game; they won the respect of people beside them and the adoration of the children playing at their feet. I was one of those children, and my grandfather was my champion.

I was ten when he asked me to give him a hand at the cabin. I felt important because he had a job for me to do. I remember standing beside him in the yard, eyeing the cabin up and down, one hand in my pocket, the other on a sledge-hammer that was too heavy to lift.

"Are we going to tear it down, Pop?"

He tapped the bib of my baseball cap playfully and

answered, "No, Gem, we're going to build it back up again."

And with that, he took the sledgehammer away and put a hammer in my hand, grabbed a handful of nails from the tobacco tin on the ground, and showed me how to put them to wood.

Not long after, a few of his friends dropped by. Some came with tools, while others showed up carrying lumber. By the end of the day, the job was done, and we all had a hand in it. This memory has become a blueprint for all of my community work.

When my grandfather was dying of cancer, I'd visit him in the hospital and take him for a little stroll down the corridor. My arm tightly fastened around his tiny waist as his arm clutched my shoulder. He clung to me as if his life depended on it. And in those moments, I guess it did. The night before he died, he was experiencing a lot of pain, more than usual. He tottered as we walked. It took an incredible amount of effort for him to put one foot in front of the other.

"Do you want to take a break, Pop?"

"I won't win first place, Gem, but I'll cross the finish line," he answered.

I never forgot that. In fact, I clung to his words as I walked the loneliest stretches of the Trans-Canada. Whenever I couldn't summon up enough drive to keep putting one foot in front of the other, because I had no skin left on the heels of my feet, I held on to that moment and pushed onward.

A half an hour after we started our walk down the hospital corridor, we finally made it back to his bed. He went to sleep and never woke up. Two weeks before he died, he told my father he'd be with his wife on their anniversary, and he died that very day.

W.H. Auden's poem "Funeral Blues" opens with a command: "Stop all the clocks." And that's exactly how I felt when my grandfather died. I felt the whole world should have to stop to honour this one man. I felt, deeply and intimately, that time had stopped as the path before me curled into a question mark.

Sometime in the weeks before his death, as weak as he was, he managed to write a letter to my father with instructions about what to do once he died. His handwriting was always far from perfect because, as a boy, his teachers, the Christian Brothers, forced him to write with his right hand instead of his natural left.

In his will, he left his pocket watch to me—that golden timepiece symbolic of all his hard work and loyalty. And it still keeps perfect time.

LESSON

PART ONE

The professor's cool demeanor awakened a boyish curiosity within me the moment she entered the classroom. My gaze latched on to the rhythm of her step as she patrolled the front of the room. She began the lecture by defining colonialism as the conquest and control of other people, their lands and goods. Seemed fitting given that I had my mind set on learning the ways in which she herself could be conquered. I found her incredibly attractive, both physically and intellectually. But as time went on, I learned my lesson—what she really taught me was how to conquer myself.

I had a lot to prove. My academic record was spotty at best. My sexual-abuse case had been settled outside of court, and I felt removed from the entire process. My age situated me between a mother who declared the settlement would be used for tuition and a lawyer who insisted the trial would be too traumatic. Although they had my best interests in mind, all I wanted was an opportunity to tell the priest that what he took from me could never be bought. As an act of rebellion, I gave the settlement money away and sabotaged my undergraduate courses.

Years later, after undergoing therapy to help me work through the sexual abuse I suffered, I decided to take my life back. Part of that process involved applying to graduate school, and as a veteran activist, Gender Studies seemed to be the best fit. In order to get accepted, however, I had to get an A in Post-colonialism—a course she happened to be teaching.

She passed a sheet of paper around and invited us to write down our names and pronoun preferences. When the sheet landed on my desk, I quickly scribbled she/her next to my name without even thinking twice—I was only ever taught to think once.

And I was distracted. Her shoes were indigo—shoes that could be mistaken for boots. *What distinguishes shoes from boots?* I wondered. *Can a shoe be a boot or a boot a shoe? And where do sandals fit within the footwear spectrum...outside of the obvious placement on the bottoms of one's feet?* My mind was everywhere...

"If colonialism impacts all aspects of our being, how do we provide a full inquiry into our ability to question it?" she asked. Trusting the arch of her back to the oak desk lodged in the center of the room, she chased her question with a stiff quote from Audre Lorde: "The master's tools will never dismantle the master's house."

I forgot about her boots and found my footing.

– – – – –

Her arms folded into one another like the petals of a rose that had forgotten how to bloom. I sought to unravel her, to travel her like a winding road and release her wings.

"Hegemony is a continual process because resistance to power is achieved through a combination of coercion and consent, i.e., resistance to power impacts power," she stated. My mind jumped backwards to my childhood.

Growing up on a street full of boys, as the only girl, I was often teased and sexually bullied. One day, even though I was still very little, my brain grew bigger, and I decided to dress like a boy. I remember pulling my grandfather's footstool into the bathroom, closing the door quickly without making a sound, and checking to make sure the lock was secure. Placing the stool in front of the small rectangular mirror situated above the sink, I proudly stood up to myself for the first time. I remember feeling good about the clothes I had on, which became my second, much more durable, skin.

I was assigned a gender on the day I was born, and from that moment on, I felt like I was living a lie. I had no word for it, of course, but I felt it. My mother didn't like it when I played sports, even though I was athletically inclined. At the time, she believed that only boys did that, whereas girls should be more concerned with appearances. I hated when she'd make me put on a dress. Dresses prevented me from climbing trees, not to mention made me more accessible to the boys on the street. The bottom part of a dress, for example, when purposely placed over the face prevents someone from looking you directly in the eye; it also triggers a feeling of suffocation. I liken it to drowning, except you're still able to breathe, as much as you lack the will to continue to do so at that moment. I still have trouble breathing in small spaces.

– – – – –

Wide eyed, I watched her pace back and forth the classroom, picking up speed with each new idea. Her aquamarine skirt collapsed like a wave as she paused abruptly to review her notes set out on the podium.

It's ironic that every girl I had a crush on in high school wore skirts, and I hated wearing dresses. When I'd dream of girls back then, I imagined I was a boy. I didn't want to be a lesbian because the church taught that homosexuality was a sin.

"Anne McClintock offers critiques on postcolonial theory and refers to the danger and pitfalls of using binaries to view the world," she asserted.

As soon as class ended, I quickly collected myself, along with my books, in an attempt to beat my classmates in the race towards her.

"Are you going to the Take Back The Night March," I inquired. Hoping to impress her, I added, "I'm giving the keynote, and you've inspired my speech."

I immediately searched her face in anticipation. Surprised, she smiled and nodded her head in favour. Not giving her the chance to speak, I told her I'd see her there and rushed off, pretending to have another commitment. As if anything would be more appealing than listening to her. Her words and gestures were key—I could feel my mind open.

– – – – –

I paraded across the concrete platform as if I owned the place. I knew she was watching. I had spotted her during the march.

"Are there any feminists in the *h-o-u-s-e*?" I hollered. And the crowd roared.

I took my place behind the podium and proceeded to address the hundreds of women gathered at the steps of City Hall.

"I dedicate this speech to my professor" I stated. "This one's for you, Doc. Hope I get an A."

She was in my classroom now.

The theories of Audre Lorde and Michel Foucault in confluence with my grandmother's praxis were the foundation of my speech. For instance, we may not be able to use the master's tools to dismantle the master's house because institutions informed by the colonial encounter have constructed the societal embodiment of our individual identities, but we still have room to renovate using other tools—tools that were handed down to us by women like my grandmother. Women who, despite the strictures of gender, salvaged whatever supplies they could and built a life for themselves in spite of it all.

"On top of the ashes, I'm the master of my own house, and I like what I've built so far," I concluded.

After I was released from the assemblage of women, she was waiting with her arms outstretched.

"A-plus," she declared, her smile as wide as her arms.

"Hope you feel that way when you grade my paper because it's the same as my speech," I said with a smirk.

We laughed as we embraced and not long after went our separate ways.

– – – – –

When class ended, she handed out our papers.

"I marked the papers hard," she warned.

The softness of her manner as she called my name was like a summons to my heart. I panicked for a moment, but quickly remembered how she reacted after she heard the speech in an attempt to reassure myself. Not wanting to look at my paper in the classroom, I found a bench just outside of the Science Building and immediately skipped to the last page where her comments were written:

> C. This was an excellent speech, but in terms of your paper, I asked for five pages not four, four sources not three. You are obviously capable of digging deeper into this feminist analysis, and I look forward to seeing you do so in your next paper.

At that moment, all I felt like digging was my own grave, but instead of giving up, I dug into myself. I had no choice but to go deeper and no way of knowing what I would resurrect. By the end of the term, I had earned my A and started grad school the following semester.

PART TWO

On June 2, 2015, she was attending an academic conference in Ottawa while I was there to witness Ryan Cleary table a Private Member's Bill, which I helped draft, for an Institutional Abuse Awareness Day. Like Newfoundland and Labrador, many provinces and Indigenous communities across the country have their own horror stories of abuse. I chose June 1 because it was the date that the doors at Mount Cashel Orphanage closed for good, and it was also the beginning of National Indigenous History Month in Canada.

I invited her to join me at the House of Commons, in the MP Lounge, to watch the reading of the Bill. Once it was tabled, she accompanied Ryan Cleary and I downstairs to the press gallery where I stood up and told the entire country about Pathways, an organization I founded for survivors of religious institutional abuse because a Roman Catholic priest sexually abused me when I was young. She was in the audience during the presser, and as I stood behind the podium, directly in front of the Canadian flag, I focused on her instead of the cameras. And when I took my place on the platform this time, the only thing I owned was myself.

Later that evening, after a celebration with Ryan Cleary and his staff, we stood in the middle of Sparks Street and watched television coverage about the Truth and Reconciliation Commission's findings on a television screen through the huge glass window in the CBC Radio building—arms woven together. As "women" and islanders, our connection surpassed circumstance and could be traced along the lines of colonial oppression. We couldn't hear what the people being interviewed were saying, but their faces spoke volumes. As the country was shifting, I could feel myself shift, too. I was beginning to see things differently, and in doing so, I saw her again for the very first time, even though tears blurred my eyes at that particular moment. Her image faded from my waking dreams, allowing space for her words to take root instead. I put my aspiration for her to rest and we became friends.

The professor's lectures stayed with me as I walked. I called her from the Trans-Canada Highway after seeing a Newfoundland flag at the entrance of a park. It stood on guard, keeping watch and waving at me as I passed. The flag inspired a great sense of patriotism in me for some of the things it represented. But I also felt the need to rebel against its celebration of our colonial past, and to raise my voice in support of all the subjugated groups the flag fails to acknowledge. Reality is far more complicated than our monuments and icons would have us believe. And the complex struggle with identity doesn't end there.

The professor taught me that we are settlers within our own bodies because of the institutions that have shaped us. I realize now that the space I inhabit is the only body I can lay claim to as my own.

KING

At forty-five, my mom's father all but lost his voice to throat cancer. I only ever knew him to whisper. His voice lulled me whenever he spoke. His parents raised their seven children on Signal Hill. He was the middle child. Because he played on the hill as a boy, he always knew the best spots for picking berries. When he'd take me picking with him, he'd make me repeat the names of all the wildflowers we encountered along our path. He even told me what ones I could eat if I was ever in a bind.

"How do you know all this stuff, Pop?" I asked.

"I grew up dirt poor," he answered. "Sometimes, I ate whatever I could find."

He taught me the patterns of clouds and how to read weather, how to forge paths and find my way back if I ever got lost.

"You don't need a compass," he told me. "As long as you

have a sense of yourself and your surroundings, you'll find your way back."

Looking back, I don't think either of us knew how those words would help me now.

As we sat on a mound of grass eating a handful of berries and gazing over The Narrows from the Queen's Battery, he told me that his father had been the flagman during the First World War. If an enemy ship entered the harbour, his job was to alert soldiers by raising the flag. And because his father had to live in Queen's Battery to do that job, he was given chickens, sheep, and kerosene. He spoke with such pride as he showed me where his father would shoot the noonday gun.

When his mother, a devout Roman Catholic, married his father, a member of the Salvation Army, her family closed all the drapes in their house because she married outside of their religion. Ironically, as a teenager he was prevented from enlisting in the Second World War because all of his older brothers were already soldiers, and there was a family quota at the time. Instead, he was given a band for his arm and was tasked with going to civilian houses to ensure their drapes were blacked out at night so that no light would aid enemy aircraft.

"There are all kinds of wars," he told me. "Lines get drawn before the drapes."

I never knew what that meant until I was on the front lines of my own battles, only to realize later in life that the biggest battle I would ever face was the war I waged on myself.

Growing up in poverty couldn't have been easy for my

grandfather, but whatever hardships he faced taught him how to survive. He managed to get a job when he was seventeen at East End Bakery and made a name for himself because of his cakes. Eventually he was hired as a master baker at Walsh's Bakery. When he married my grandmother, he never moved far from the house he grew up in. They rented a house from the church on Power's Court until they received an eviction notice stating it would be demolished because a new school, which I would eventually attend, was being built. With nowhere else to go, my grandmother told the monsignor that she would offer God another baby if the church could find them a new home. He found them a small rundown house in the Battery for $32.50 per month. The floorboards were rotted, and the walls were dank. There was no hot water or electricity. My grandfather had to use a cigarette lighter when he went to view the house that evening. He moved his wife and six children in the next day with several tins of paint and a toolbox in tow. My grandmother was pregnant again not long after.

Whenever I'd stay with my grandparents, I'd wake up each morning and rush to their bedroom so I could watch my grandfather get ready. Even after he retired, he dressed to the nines. His shirt and pants were neatly pressed and laid out at the bottom of the bed each day. He'd greet me in the doorway with his soft smile in a pair of white cotton boxers and a white T-shirt, lift me up and put me on the dresser. I'd watch him get ready to shave. One morning, instead of brushing the lather from his shaving soap onto his face, he put it on my face instead. He told me to hold still as he pretended to shave me with the blunt side of the straight razor. When he finished, he wiped my face with his hand-kerchief, splashed some aftershave on his hands, and then onto my face.

"I feel like a king, Pop," I said.

"You are a king," he answered.

"But I'm not a man," I said.

He lifted my chin with his forefinger and looked me straight in the eye, "You just have to be you," he said.

He put his ascot hat on my head, gave me a wink, and told me to get ready for school. I wore his hat to school that day and tipped it to the old men gathered around the corner store as I passed by. They tipped theirs in return. You'd have to be something like a king to get a nod from the original corner boys of St. John's. I felt more like myself than ever before. I didn't take the hat off all day until just before my mother got home from work.

HOME RUN

The game was tied. It was the bottom of the seventh and the bases were loaded. Little Tom Power stands behind the softball diamond sporting a white, button-down, short-sleeved shirt, blue cotton shorts, argyle socks, and brown leather dress shoes. His tiny hands firmly gripped around the backstop mesh.

As little as he was, he'd use all his might to drag his mother by the hand to that very spot so when it was my turn at bat he could yell out, "Hit me a homerun, Gemma!" I told him I couldn't hit a homerun without him. And believe it or not, I'd hit one each time—with his help. I may have been on his sister Erin's softball team, but he was my cheerleader. Even at the age of three, his voice had purpose.

To warm up, I'd swing not one bat, but two, get down on one knee in front of him, pick up a handful of dirt and rub it between my hands before wiping them off in my uniform.

And as I stepped up to the plate, I'd point in whatever direction I was going to hit the ball. My position was centerfield, and I always batted number four—the power hitter. In the outfield, it didn't matter if I could simply reach out my glove and catch the ball, I'd still dive for it, trying to make every play look spectacular. I'd set the stage to play the crowd, but the show was always for him, my first fan.

I never felt more like a champion as I did when that little boy looked up at me, his big brown eyes swirling with wonderment as his curly blonde locks tumbled over his sweet little forehead.

One day after the game, two boys were making fun of me. I was drinking a can of Coca Cola when one of them said, "Look, the half breed even holds the can like *it's* a boy."

"I can't tell what *it* is, if it's a boy or a girl," said the other one with a snicker.

I could feel my face getting flushed. My heart beat like a drum in my chest. It didn't matter that I had just hit a grand slam and won the game: I felt like a loser.

All of a sudden, little Tom barrelled through the boys and said, "That's not an it, that's a Gemma!"

Then he turned to me and said, "Why you little Gemma," and jumped right into my arms. The boys suddenly lost interest and left me alone. Little Tom was my shield.

"Why you little Thomas," I whispered. Giggling, he jumped out of my arms and pulled me by the hand towards his sister.

We won the championship that year. I got a trophy for the most homeruns. But little Tom was my champion. And twenty-nine years later, he came to my rescue again.

Erin and I remained friends even after we aged out of the softball league, and every now and then we'd chat about what Tom was up to. In 2008, at twenty-one years of age, he became the national radio host of *Deep Roots* on CBC. And in 2011, he hosted *Radio 2 Morning*, CBC's lead morning national music program. In 2016, after guest hosting *q* on CBC Radio 1, he became the permanent host. I heard Tom's voice over the airwaves during my walk. And sometimes, in a moment of doubt, when my feet hurt so bad I could barely put one foot in front of the other, I'd think of little Tom cheering me on and remember why I was walking.

When a child looks up to you, it's an incredible feeling. It moves you to the point where you feel you can do anything. I thought about the innocence in Tom's face and the trust he placed in me. I thought about the innocent trust I had placed in others.

If someone in a position of power and trust, who stages themselves as a representative of God, abuses you, the damage is as deep in your psyche as the faith you were raised in. You never fully recover from it; you just find ways to cope. I'm one of the lucky ones because I have a certain amount of privilege: an education, a supportive network of family and friends, a good therapist, a public profile, etc. But how many people have I hurt during my long road of recovery? Thankfully I never turned to drugs or alcohol like so many other survivors, but I moved from one relationship to another because the level of intimacy long-term relationships required forced me to go to a place deep within myself that, at the time, felt unbearable. And it was only on the walk that I started to understand why.

— — — — —

Back when I was small, I thought a ghost lived in my closet. My mother had to leave the hall light on so I could fall asleep because I thought the light would drive the specter away. Soon after, I realized there were no such things as ghosts. A few years later, another ghost haunted me, but then I was the one hiding in the closet, and when I came out, the light did drive that ghost away.

We all have closets that we need to come out of. Secrets we keep inside because we're afraid or ashamed. We convince ourselves that people won't love us anymore if we tell them that we're broken or that we're hurting in ways they can't even imagine. But those fears are not always warranted. A few years ago, I came out of another closet. I told the world that I was a survivor of clergy sexual abuse. It was a leap of faith, a different kind of faith, a faith in the people around me. And you know what? No one stopped loving me. I may have been broken, but I put the pieces back together, and I am no longer haunted by shame.

I came into this world as a girl—a girl with the heart of boy, a boy whose imagination ran wild. And only in the girl's dreams was the boy allowed to play. The girl grew into a woman, and the boy fell asleep, but I'm awake now. It appears that my light is brighter than the ghost that lurked within the closet of my own body. I am haunted no more. The boy has come out to play. I am both victim and survivor, I've been both Catholic and Protestant, I've loved both men and women, and I have parts of me that are both female and male.

The song "Que Sera Sera" was often sung to me by my mother when I was little, and as much as I enjoyed listening to her voice, I'd secretly cringe when I heard the words "little girl." One day I asked her how I got my name. She told me that my father discovered the saint Gemma Galgani in a book he was reading about Christian mystics while he was studying Religious Studies at Memorial University. He wrote the name Gemma on a flat beach stone and gave it to her when she was pregnant with me. I asked her what my name would've been if I had been a boy. "Mark," she told me.

"Maybe I'll make my *mark* in other ways, Mom," I said.

– – – – –

I took my first step at eight months. And here I was, thirty-eight years later, having just taken 1,125,000 steps across the island. I was in the homestretch with only thirty kilometers left to go. The journey felt much longer than 908 kilometers because of the distance I travelled within myself—no amount of training could have prepared me for that.

My friends Andrea Power and Steve Kent joined me for that homestretch, and as we moved along the predetermined route, random people began to join us as we walked. By the time we climbed Kenna's Hill, we must have had more than thirty people alongside us. Cars were honking jubilantly as they passed by. We could see the hundreds of people gathered at the Mount Cashel Memorial even before we reached Elizabeth Avenue. As I approached the Sobeys parking lot, Pamela Morgan's song, "Pathways," blared over the loud speakers. Media trucks encircled the crowd. My eyes may have been filled with tears, but I was elated to see so many people standing there, a kind of celebratory defiance on the unholy grounds where Mount Cashel once stood.

My mother was the first to embrace me, and then a little girl and boy presented me with wildflowers. One by one, people lined up to greet me. One woman threw the New-foundland flag over my head and tied it around my neck.

"My brothers were hurt at Mount Cashel, and I lost them to suicide," she said. "You walked hope home to me. You're a hero."

Peter Soucy emceed the event. Des Walsh wrote a poem to mark the occasion. Mark Hiscock sang the "Ode to Newfoundland." Steve Kent brought greetings on behalf of the provincial government. Nicole Keiley spoke about the Sexual Assault Crisis and Prevention Centre, and Dr. Patricia Dold spoke about Pathways. Three representatives of various Christian denominations spoke: Father Paul Lundrigan (Catholic), Reverend Heather Sanford (United), and Dr. David Bell (Anglican). In addition to representing his church, David, my former professor and dear friend, was tasked with introducing me. I made my way to the podium and delivered this speech:

Mount Cashel Memorial Address
Sunday, August 2, 2015

Friends,

On July 2, 2015, I began my walk across Newfoundland in the lovely little town of Port aux Basques ending it here in St. John's at the Mount Cashel Memorial. And not only did I walk across the fifteenth largest island in the world, I walked across the most beautiful island in the world.

Newfoundland poet Al Pittman, one of my favourite poets, who like Des Walsh, the poet who wrote a poem commemorating this event, wrote from a sense of place. He once described Newfoundland as "an island in the sky," and I couldn't agree more. Having walked across it, cooling my face and mouth beside its tumbling brooks, inhaling the scent of its wildflowers and trees, discovering the might of its mountains, roaring my name across its valleys waiting for its return and basking in the buoyant glow of the people who dwell here, I know it's a place like no other—a place above all others, high up in the sky to be wished upon like stars.

I knew it would be challenging to walk over 900 kilometers in such a short timeframe, but I also knew that I would do it. Why? Because I'm from Newfoundland and Labrador, and if there's anything we know how to do, it's how to survive.

I'm a survivor in every sense of the word. No matter what crosses my path in life, I keep on going. This walk is a metaphor for us all.

In spite of the blisters, the hives, the rashes, the chafing, the insect bites, the sun and wind burn. In spite of the torrential rains and monumental wind gusts. In spite of myself, I put one foot in front of the other and kept on going.

I walked to the other side of a storm and rested beneath a rainbow. I gazed into the eyes of a coyote without fear because I have faced my greatest fear—myself.

I went from holding a grown man as he cried,

whose father was abused by a priest, to waltzing with an elderly woman on a highway shoulder who was abused at Belvedere Orphanage. I've heard so many sad stories that I started to pray again because I didn't know what else to do for people, except walk and pray, walk and pray.

I heard so many stories while on the road. Today, however, I am here to remind you of one story in particular – a story that we'd like to forget, but we must never forget. That's why I ended my walk at this memorial.

1989 was the year the Mount Cashel scandal erupted, leaving deep wounds in our province. Since that time, numerous cases of abuse have been reported, and there are an untold number of cases that have been settled silently, outside of court. Mine was one of those cases, but I have broken the silence and, in doing so, can only hope to have created the space for others to do the same. No more guilt and no more shame!

And we mustn't forget residential school survivors from Labrador who were excluded from the Conservative government's federal apology. And then there are other provinces and Indigenous communities elsewhere in Canada who have their own horror stories of abuse. First Nations, Innu, and Métis children were taken from their families and forced to attend residential schools over much of the last century, and there are an estimated 80,000 survivors of these schools alive today. Even

*after the Truth and Reconciliation Commission,
the intergenerational trauma of such a tragedy
continues to this day.*

*Although Mount Cashel is just one example of the
rampant abuse that occurred within religious-run
institutions, it's the tragedy that precipitated a
turning point in awareness of this form of abuse.
By ending the walk at that site, I want us to
reclaim this space, while paying respects to the
many men who made the tragic journey from their
homes to the orphanage. Their names are not
included on the memorial, but we will honour
them by working to ensure that abuse of this kind,
of any kind, never happens again. That will be
our living memorial to them.*

*We are all products of the institutions we were
raised in. They have influenced the way we think,
what we believe, and the way we treat one another,
and because of that, we have just as much to
unlearn as we do to learn.*

*Mount Cashel was one of the darkest chapters in
our province's collective past. We can't rewrite that
story, but we can change how it ends.*

Thank you.

Before Andrea and Steve joined me for the last twenty
kilometers of that walk, I reflected on my journey as I spent
the morning walking alone. Like the poet Robert Frost in
"The Road Not Taken," I've stumbled upon forks in the road.
Sometimes, I've been conflicted because both paths appealed

to me. And there were times when I've vowed to come back to other routes, other tasks, but then never had the chance. Using the common analogy of life as a journey, Frost wonders how different his life would have been had he taken another direction. But we can't go back. We can only move forward. Frost's poem suggests that we sometimes make arbitrary or uninformed choices and then seek to validate those choices later, through hindsight, and that those subsequent self-justifications for the life we've lived can sometimes be founded on self-deception.

Even though we've been conditioned to think in binaries—male and female, gay and straight, Catholic and Protestant, etc.—those divisions are more about social control than about self-discovery or self-awareness. Sometimes two roads diverge, and you choose neither, because you have to make your own honest path. We have the power to claim and, in some cases, reclaim ourselves, to chart a new course and invite others to either follow along or make their own way. Some roads are longer than others, some rougher. Sometimes the longest and roughest road you'll ever travel is the one that leads you back to yourself.

ACKNOWLEDGMENTS

There are many people who deserve my heartfelt thanks for their unconditional love and steadfast support.

First and foremost, thanks to my wonderful wife, Rebecca. After a decade of friendship, we began a new chapter in our lives by living our very own love story.

There's an old African proverb, "It takes a village to raise a child." Well, that certainly applies to me. I'd like to thank my mother, Lynda, for all the sacrifices she made to give me the best chance at life, for showing me grace when I didn't deserve it, and for being the first person to teach me how to challenge the status quo. My father, Frank, introduced me to literature, sports, politics, and rock and roll, and taught me how to own my life, both good and bad. My late step-father, David, taught me how to cook and play golf, and always stepped up without ever having to be asked. My step-brothers Ian and Blair helped clean up after all my parties (I had a lot of parties, so it's worth the mention) and showed me that, when it comes to blood and water, love is the thickest of all. And to my aunts, uncles, and cousins in both my immediate and extended families from the Hayward, Hickey, and Kirkland clans, I never take for granted how lucky I am to be embraced by such a huge, fun-loving circle.

Thank you to my grandparents Agnes Hickey (née Power) and Gerald Hickey, and Mary Hayward (née Duffy) and James Hayward—my heroes.

I want to express my deep gratitude to all of the teachers and professors who have challenged and inspired me over the years, especially Dr. Vicki Hallett, my supervisor, who helped me recognize my intellectual worth and rocked my entire worldview.

I'd like to thank the incredible team at Breakwater Books: Rebecca Rose, Donna Francis, Rhonda Molloy, Samantha Fitzpatrick, and my editor James Langer, whose eyes have the precision of a sharp shooter when it comes to editing. Words cannot express my appreciation for his professional advice during the polishing of this manuscript.

David Howells, my favourite photographer on the planet, waived his fee for my author photo and donated the cover image as well.

My Hope Walk could not have been accomplished without the help of the Hope Walk Committee: Charmaine Davidage, Janet Harron, Travis White, Greg Knott and Jennifer Walsh.

Dr. Patricia Dold, Dr. Dorothy Vaandering, Raelene Lee, and Deborah Thomas who were board members of Pathways during the walk.

Special thanks to Justin Halley, my right-hand man; my drivers, John Hayward and Clayton Handrigan for having my back; and my powerhouse training team: TA Loeffler, Shane Monahan, Philip Alcock, Audrey Hynes, Xi Hong, and Colleen Dunn.

Huge shout out to the Newfoundland and Labrador Sexual Assault Crisis and Prevention Center, Coastline Consultants, and VOCM for the generous in-kind donations, support, and partnership.

Thanks to The Royal Canadian Mounted Police and the Royal Newfoundland Constabulary for having my back, and to the municipalities, organizations, student groups, and parks for the warm welcome and tremendous hospitality.

The walk could never have occurred without our generous sponsors: The Provincial Government of Newfoundland and Labrador, the Mennonite Central Committee, Budden and Associates, A1 Automotive, Bob Buckingham Law, the Ellsworth Group of Companies, Lansing Properties, and the Archdiocese of St. John's.

Thank you to Hickman Motors, Northshore Roofing, Eastcom, The Travel Bug, Alpine Country Lodge, The Healthy Vibe, the Bennett Group of Companies, Sobeys, and Dominion for donating goods and services I needed on the road.

Josh Eddy of the *Outport Magazine* and Chad Pelley of *The Overcast* provided much needed free advertising space.

Thanks to Vanessa Stockley of Granite Studios for the wicked graphic design; Jenny Smith of Ray Agency for the deadly ad campaign; and Paul Hayward of First Focus Productions for the best promotional video of all time.

And thanks to all my favourite local haunts for helping out with the fundraising campaign: Fogtown Barber and Shop, Rocket Bakery, The Club, Yellowbelly Brewery, The Sprout, and Living Planet.

Des Walsh, Duane Andrews, Lynda Boyd and Chris Evans for taking part in a photo shoot to promote the walk and the late Gerald Squires for donating his image.

Big thanks to the folks who walked alongside me, for their support and the gift of their company: Shane Monahan (146 kms), Audrey Hynes (42 kms) Lynda Hayward (40 kms), TA Loeffler (28 kms), Steve Kent (20 kms), Andrea Power (20 kms), Raelene Lee (20 kms), Philip Alcock (10 kms), Jennifer Lokash (10 kms), Ryan Cleary (10 kms), Andrew Parsons (10 kms), Sandy Collins (5 kms), Tina Learning (2.5 kms), Gina Keeping (2.5 kms), Natelle Tulk (2.5 kms), Trina Kennedy (1.5 kms).

To all of my friends and supporters who follow me every step of the way, I love you.

GEMMA HICKEY is a passionate humanist whose activism has changed the legal landscape of Canada, expanding rights, equality and dignity for the LGBTQ2+ community and raising awareness for survivors of clergy abuse. Gemma became a well-known force for change when they co-led the movement that legalized same-sex marriage in Canada in 2005. In 2017, their request for a gender-neutral birth certificate spurred Newfoundland and Labrador to change its law, and Gemma became the first person in Canada to receive a non-binary birth certificate and one of the first Canadians to receive a gender-neutral passport.

In addition to their volunteer work with Pathways, since 2010 Gemma has been the Executive Director of Artforce (formerly For the Love of Learning), a charity that works to create new paths for at-risk youth by fostering literacy and creative skills. In 2012, Gemma was recognized with a Queen's Diamond Jubilee Medal for their contribution to human rights in Canada. In 2016, Gemma was named a Newfoundland and Labrador Human Rights Champion.

Gemma's physical and personal journey through gender transformation is the subject of the documentary *Just Be Gemma*. The film first aired on CBC television and the Documentary Channel in 2017 and was screened at various Canadian film festivals in 2018 and made its international debut in Tokyo, Japan, in 2019. A strong believer in ongoing learning and individual growth, Gemma is presently a master's candidate in Gender Studies at Memorial University and lives in St. John's.

AUTHOR PHOTO: DAVID HOWELLS